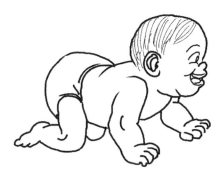

DEBUT DADS – THE FIRST SEASON OF
FATHERHOOD

BY ALEX GOSS

DAD FC: DEBUT DADS
THE FIRST SEASON OF FATHERHOOD

Designed by Nathalie Baude
Illustrations and artwork by Congchen Saelee
Copyright © Alex Goss, 2016. Alex Goss has asserted his right to be identified as the author of this work in accordance with the Copyright, Designs and Patent Act 1998.

First Published in 2016
Second edition 2017

www.dadfc.com
www.facebook.com/DadFC

ACKNOWLEDGEMENTS

I want to say a huge thanks to everyone involved in motivating me and helping me create this book. Without you, I'd have just put it off and put it off and put it off before regretting never having written in. First, massive thanks go to my wife, Nathalie, who has given me the time and freedom to sit in our tiny study and write this book. A big thanks has to go to my daughter too – without her, I'd be lost. She defines me now.

Very special thanks to Steff, Chris and Bridget for spending their time to check and approve the content of this book. Your expertise and advice are always very much appreciated. This book is much better because of you three.

I extend further thanks to all those who've shared their ideas and suggestions with me throughout the period of me writing this, including Scott, Seb, Kirsty, Stu, Caroline, George, Piotr, Neil, James, Mark I (for the idea for the cover!), Ranj, Chad, Kev and Tim.

I'm grateful to all the Dad FC fans on social media, especially those fans on Facebook. This book is written for all of you and all of your friends, family and the dads-to-be that you ever know. If this book helps one dad with one tiny bit of parenting, then I'm a happy author.

Thank you

CONTENTS

Chapter 1 - Introduction 1

Chapter 2 - Pre-Season... 5
Get the stadium kitted out 6
    Your bedroom.. 6
    Baby's bedroom (or Theatre of Dreams) 7
    Baby changing 8
    Breastfeeding & bottle feeding........................... 8
    Bathroom 9
    Baby clothes.. 11
    Buy a couple of 'tiny baby' or 'early baby' onesies.... 11
    Front room 12
    Physio room 12
    The bed options 13
    Travelling to away games.................................... 15
    Choosing whether or not to use a dummy?......... 15
Get the stadium ready... 17
    Freeze meals in preparation 17
    Adopt a high standard of cleaning and sterilise stuff...... 17
    Draft a cleaner into the club 18
    Practice your set pieces...................................... 20
From the terraces
    "What does it feel like to become a dad?" 21
Post match interview:
    "I'd completely lost her"................................... 22

Chapter 3 - Making your debut 25
What to think about once your baby is born 26
    Set Piece 1 - The best ways to hold a newborn baby...... 27
    First decision: Vitamin K and the medical.......... 30
    What will my baby look like?............................. 31
    You'll get a little red book about your baby's health....... 32

Set Piece 2 - Driving your baby home 32

What to think about at home **33**

Before the first bottle feed – sterilise everything 33

Set piece 3 - Bottle feeding 36

Set piece 4 - Winding 38

Set piece 5 - Changing nappies – tackling dirty 39

Set piece 6 - Bathing – hitting the showers 42

Umbilical cord 45

Cutting nails 45

From the terraces

When should I give my baby his first bath? 46

How many times a week should I bathe my baby? 46

Crying **47**

Most common reasons your baby might be crying 47

Things to help your baby stop crying 48

Meeting the fans and press **49**

Pundits 49

Glory supporters 49

Die-hard fans 50

Police presence at today's game 50

From the terraces

"How soon should we have visitors round?" 51

"When should we invite the family round?" 51

Post-match interview **52**

Chapter 4 - Sleep and 3am Kick Offs **55**

Putting the baby into bed **56**

Safety first 56

How to lay them down 57

What a baby should wear in bed 58

A rough idea of how they might sleep as they grow 58

Sleep routines 59

Example of an enjoyable routine for both of you 60

Make the baby's room a theatre of dreams 60

Make your baby comfortable 62

Crying in the night 63
Dad's sleep and sleep deprivation 66
From the terraces
"Should I let my baby cry at night?" 70
"When should I put my baby in their own room?" 71
Post-match interview 72

Chapter 5 - Baby v. Food 73
Milk...74
Breast feeding and its benefits 74
What are the benefits of bottle feeding? 75
Combining breast and bottle milk 75
How do I know if they've had enough milk? 76
What actually is formula milk?...................77
Should I give my baby water?....................77
Solid foods and weaning 78
When is my baby ready for solids? 78
How will my baby react to solid foods? 79
What solids food should I try? 79
How much solid food should I give my baby?.............80
Starting line-up | 1st team of solids 81
Manager's tactics 83
Vitamins...84
Kit needed 84
Food safety & hygiene 85
Tricks for feeding a baby 86
Post-match interview 88

Chapter 6 - Travel and Away Games.................. 91
Planning away games................................92
Travel bag and changing bag essentials 92
Car-seat safety....................................93
Plan & pack with the 5 Ws & H Model 94
When can a baby leave the house for the first time? 96
What sort of trips should we go on?.................97

Accommodation 98
Pushchair or Pram? The options 99
Pram...100
Pushchair..100
Two-in-one travel system 100
Three-in-one travel system 100
Buggy 100
Stroller...101
Some scenarios to think about when choosing travel
equipment.. 101
Other things to think about when choosing a pram?...102
Strollers on a plane....................................103
Post match interview............................104

Chapter 7 - Relationship with the Head Coach . 105
Early months..106
How will my partner feel in the first few weeks?..........108
How can a new dad help a new mum? 110
Later months 111
Arguments..111
Date her...113
Sex..114
And by the end of the first year?......................115

Chapter 8 - You: Manager of Dad FC............... 117
Becoming daddy 118
Mental wellbeing 121
Challenges vs. How to deal with them 122
Stress with tantrums..................................122
Going to work 125
Physical wellbeing...................................126
Tactics for eating (and drinking) better 127
Tactics for exercising more 127
Crazy Gang approach to parenting 128
Play dirty 130

Prioritise the important stuff and cut the crap............131
Play the long-ball and cut out the middle man...........133
Get things done in a lean way 134
Master the set pieces 135
Be 'lucky' 136
From the terraces
"Can dads get post-natal depression?" 137

Chapter 9 - Injury time....................................... **139**
He's taken a knock! Bring on the physio!..................**140**
The Dad F.C doctor's kit bag (your first aid kit) 141
What do I plan to do, if my baby... ....**142**
...has got a high temperature 142
...is having a fit, convulsion, has turned blue, rigid
or floppy..143
...is choking 144
...has had a bump or bruise 145
...has suffered a cut..145
...has swallowed tablets or medicines she shouldn't
have been taking 146
...has swallowed a poisonous chemical or a small battery
(like the small, round silver ones) 147
...has got something stuck up her nose or in her ear....147
...has suffered a burn 147
...has broken a bone 148
Colds, flu, sickness & colic **148**
Colds 149
Cough 149
Croup 150
Ear infection 150
Colic..151
From the terraces
"How do you know if your baby has colic, reflux or gas?". 153
"When do you get immediate medical help?".............153
Baby-proofing...**154**

The manager's office 154
The penalty box 154
Kitchen & cafeteria...155
Showers 155
Ready to start baby proofing?....................................155

Chapter 10 - The Loan System (Childcare) 157
Balancing work, childcare and money 158
Survive on just one salary alone? 158
Questions to ask yourself before
interviewing childminders **161**
Useful questions to ask when interviewing childminders163
Finances..**165**
Things to look out for when you visit a childminder 167

Chapter 11 - Bonding with Baby 169
Provide what they need to thrive................................170
Being what my baby needs me to be 171
Ways to bond with your baby 174
From the terraces
"How long will it take before I have a connection
with my baby?" 176
"When do you get immediate medical help?".............176
"What if I don't feel I have this connection?" 177
"How quickly can we communicate with our baby girl?" . 177

Chapter 12 - The Big Games of the Season
(Baby Development) 179
Day 1-2 – Kick-off...180
Week 1 – Set pieces...181
Week 2 – Getting to know each other........................181
Week 3 – Recovery on track.......................................182
Week 4 – Noises 184
Month 2 – Smiles and sleepless nights 184
Month 3 – Building strength 186

Month 4 – Improving skills and awareness.................187
Month 5 – Having a laugh...188
Month 6 – Teething and solids...................................189
Month 7 – Repeat, Repeat, Repeat 191
Month 8 – Crawling?..192
Month 9 – More food. Maybe more 'No's..................193
Month 10 – Improving core strength and vocab 194
Month 11 – Books and tantrums................................195
Month 12 – First steps?...195

Chapter 13 - Win it like Leicester City 197

The Final Whistle... 203

01. INTRODUCTION

"...it literally explodes..."

Jamie Redknapp

To kick things off, I'd like to say congratulations! If you've picked up this book, I'm guessing that you're either going to become a father in the not too distant future, or you're already a new dad! This book is written for you. If you're neither of these two things then I presume you're an avid fan of books for new dads, or perhaps you know someone who's becoming a new dad soon? Well, congratulations to you too; you've come to the right place.

The goal of this book is to guide new dads through the first year of parenting via useful tips, real-life anecdotes and invaluable words of wisdom. *Debut Dads: The First Season of Fatherhood* tackles parenting from pre-season to debut day, then all the way through to clinching the title (or perhaps just surviving) at the end of the campaign.

We'll be focussing on the subjects which are most important to dads: from tactics, tips and tricks that can be practiced with ease, to more detailed answers to the big questions all new dads have. We cover everything in the first year of fatherhood, including preparation before the baby arrives to successfully changing nappies, bottle feeding and bathing a baby with ease (all the regular set pieces). We'll also delve into the deeper aspects of the first season, such as coping with sleep (or the lack of it), travelling smoothly with a baby and managing a new little family.

There are tons of parenting books covering pregnancy and labour, which are almost entirely written for a mum-to-be. There's room for helping dads with the pregnancy and labour stages of parenthood too, but the big game-changing moment for dads is after their baby is born, when life completely changes forever.
So this book has been written to help dads from day 1, when their little one makes their debut in the world, and it's a dad's job to coach them through it.

There'll be amazing moments of glorious jubilation and there'll be nail-biting tension in the wee small hours of the night.

From the moment your baby exits the tunnel and takes their first steps into the Stadium of Life, *you* become Manager of Dad FC and *you* are responsible for nurturing this bright new talent.

Let's be straight with each other from the outset: This book is not for the fair-weather father. This book is for new coaches - new coaches who want to get their hands dirty in nappies, new coaches who will embrace getting soaked by the spit of little dribblers and new coaches who will welcome extra time and penalties. Welcome to Dad F.C.

CONTRACT

Title:......... **Manager of Dad FC**
Contract term:.....................**Life**
Working hours:.......**24/7/365**
Salary:.................**£0,000,000**

Name...
Signed...
Date...

_____

How to use this book

This book is split into the different areas you'll cover in the first year of fatherhood. It's designed so you can get yourself warmed up and fully prepared for your debut by reading the first few chapters, and then thumb through each chapter as and when you need to throughout the first 12 months of your baby's life. It's packed with useful content for you to refer to on an ad hoc basis.

Most chapters kick off with a narrative to get you in the zone, followed by a run-down of the key areas, tips and suggestions. We also field questions *from the terraces* (usually questions from new dads). Each chapter then ends with a post-match interview from an experienced manager, to give you comment on what it's really like to go through each stage of the first season.

I've tried not to fill this book with forced analogies – I sometimes refer to a manager or coach (meaning Dad) and a footballer or star striker (meaning Baby).

I hope you find it packed full useful things to help you on your journey to becoming a seasoned dad.

This book is approved by
- Midwife: Steff Wright
- Psychologist: Bridget Saddler Bsc (Hons) and MBPsS The British Psychological Society

02. PRE–SEASON

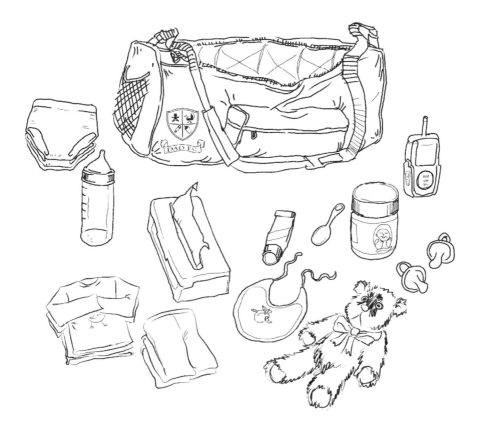

"Fail to prepare, prepare to fail"

Roy Keane

(and just about every manager or coach who's ever lived).

They say that nothing can prepare you for becoming a dad.

In that case, why not just sit back, relax and let things take their course? Whilst you don't know exactly how it will feel to become a parent for the first time, preparing for the big day can give you confidence and save you running around like a headless chicken after the birth.

The 2 key areas to tackle when it comes to preparing for the new arrival are:

> 1. Get the stadium (your home) kitted out: cot, bedding, clothes, equipment etc.
> 2. Get the stadium ready: baby-safe, tidy and clean

GET THE STADIUM KITTED OUT

YOUR BEDROOM

It's time to de-clutter fella. Make room for your new baby but don't let the little one take complete control of the place (at least not before they're actually born). You won't want this room to become a baby room or you'll lose the chance of rekindling any sort of romance any time soon.

You're going to need:

> ☑ 1 Moses basket or carry cot
> ☑ 1 mattress for the Moses basket or carry cot (firm, not soft and fits perfectly with no gaps)
> ☑ 2-3 fitted sheets
> ☑ 2-3 light blankets

☑ 1-2 baby sleeping bags

BABY'S BEDROOM (OR THEATRE OF DREAMS)

You will want your baby's bedroom to become a theatre of dreams – calming, tranquil and conducive for drifting off into the land of nod (much like Manchester United's Theatre of Dreams then). You can get more detailed tips on sleeping in chapter 4, but here are basics that you're going to need for preparing a baby's room:

☑ 1 cot or cot-bed
☑ 1 mattress for the cot or crib (firm, not soft and fits the cot perfectly with no gaps)
☑ 2-4 fitted sheets
☑ 2-3 light blankets
☑ 1 dresser
☑ 1 rocking chair (for feeding in the night and reading bedtime stories)
☑ 1 pair of black-out curtains (we also used a draft excluder to sit the curtains onto the window sill – this helps shut out daylight and any drafts – also effective if you have a heater just below the window)

BABY CHANGING

- ☑ Several packs of nappies (for newborns)
- ☑ 2 x packs of nappy bags
- ☑ 1 x nappy stacker (stores nappies and attaches to cot – optional but handy)
- ☑ 1 x changing mat
- ☑ 1 x changing table
- ☑ 6 packs of wipes (non alcoholic)
- ☑ 1-2 bags of cotton wool (for cleaning the baby's bum)
- ☑ 1 x tub of nappy cream (for use after a couple of weeks)

BREASTFEEDING & BOTTLE FEEDING

- ☑ 3 nursing bras (for sympathy)
- ☑ Some breast pads (if you're into that kind of thing)
- ☑ 1 breast pump (useful if mum is expressing)
- ☑ 1 tub of nipple cream (OK...)
- ☑ 6 bottles
- ☑ 6 teats (with a slow flow)
- ☑ 1-2 bottle brushes (for cleaning the feeding equipment before sterilising)
- ☑ A tub of infant formula (if the mum isn't breastfeeding or expressing breast milk)
- ☑ Steriliser: Make a choice between cold water, boiling water or steam sterilising. More info on these 3 options can be found in chapter 3.

BATHROOM

☑ Baby bath tub (or a washing up bowl will do)
☑ 1 soft sponge
☑ 2-3 soft towels or hooded towels
☑ 1-2 bottles of baby oils or baby bathing lotions (only for when they're more than 1 month old)

TIP

Muslin squares are the gods of the first year of fatherhood. They are the most versatile piece of kit you can have in your locker. Baby dribble, spilt milk, discrete breastfeeding, extra blanket layer, you name it – muslin squares have got it covered. Get loads of them.

Baby dribble

Discrete breastfeeding

Extra blanket layer

Spilt milk

BABY CLOTHES

- ☑ 5-7 babygros (or onesies). That's 5-7 in total for both day and night or 3-4 for day and add 2-3 sleep-suits in the night
- ☑ 5-7 vests or bodysuits. Get a mix of long-sleeved and short-sleeved
- ☑ 5-7 pairs of socks
- ☑ 2-3 cardigans (go for the soft and close-knit ones rather than cardigans with loads of holes in – in case your baby has sharp nails that can get caught in them).
- ☑ 1 or 2 hats (for cold weather but also for sunshine if you take your baby outside)
- ☑ 1 or 2 mittens (great for stopping them scratching in the night)
- ☑ 1 or 2 booties (little shoes for little people)
- ☑ 1 hooded baby jacket or a pram-suit

BUY A COUPLE OF 'TINY BABY' OR 'EARLY BABY' ONESIES

Everyone always thinks their partner is going to give birth to Neville Southall, Kevin Pressman or Abedayo Akinfenwa, when in reality a Juninho, Aaron Lennon or a Mini Messi is often the case. Friends and family also tend to buy clothes that they want to have a chance of seeing their beloved grandchild, nephew or niece wearing, so they choose things a little bigger that'll last longer. So get a 'tiny baby' outfit on the shopping list.

Oh, and go for cotton over polyester every time. It's more breathable, natural and kinder on your baby's skin.

FRONT ROOM

☑ 1 baby monitor (we recommend the CCTV with temperature version). Whilst it's a matter of personal preference, getting a baby monitor with CCTV and a temperate monitor allows you to keep a close eye on your baby and their comfort, without having to disturb them. These nifty little gadgets also come with Voice, so you can freak-out your baby by talking to them through the monitor. It's not wise to do this whilst they're sleeping (that's effectively suicide for you), but great fun when mum is in the baby room, half way through changing a nappy and completely unaware that you're watching their every move... *cue evil laugh*

☑ 1-2 blankets or shawls (to wrap the baby in)

☑ 1 baby bouncer (which can be used from birth)

☑ 1 breast feeding pillow or cushion (optional but useful for supporting your baby during feeding)

PHYSIO ROOM

☑ A good First aid book and medical references

☑ First aid kit: see chapter 9 for more info on what goes in a first-aid kit

☑ In-ear thermometer

☑ Baby syringe (usually included with the medicine)

☑ Get local GP and NHS numbers into your phone book. Bookmark the NHS site on your phone. Bookmark the local Chinese takeaway whilst you're at it.

☑ Paracetamol liquid medicine (which can be used from 2-3 months old)

THE BED OPTIONS

One of the big (and by 'big' I mean 'expensive') things I wish I was given some decent advice on is the difference between all of the bed options for a newborn baby. There seems to be loads of choice, all looking pretty different to each other, with each one serving the same purpose (sleep). Each one sells itself as the perfect solution. So here's the lowdown on the options:

Bed: That's what you sleep in

Cot-bed: Can be slept in from debut to 2-3 years old. A cot that converts into a small bed for a toddler (i.e. the side bars can be removed and its height-adjustable).

Cot: Can be slept in from debut to 2-3 years old. These are height-adjustable and are much bigger than cribs. You may not have room for a cot in your own bedroom. Health experts recommend that your baby sleeps in the same room as you for the first 6 months.

Crib: Can be slept in from debut to 4-6 months old (or until your baby can push themselves onto their hands and knees unaided). Cribs rock from side to side which can help the baby sleep.

Cradle: This is effectively the same as a crib. See Crib.

Moses basket: Can be slept in from debut to 3 months. Moses baskets are secure, snug and lightweight. They are usually made from wicker and have handles to help you move the basket around the house. Moses baskets are more snug than a cot but can only be used until about 3 months. Stands (including rocking stands) can be bought for Moses baskets.

Bassinet: This is effectively a Moses basket and commonly comes with a stand. See Moses basket.

Carry cot: Often come as part of a pram. These can be used from birth.

Co-sleeper: Can be slept in from debut to 4-6 months old. This is a crib that can be attached to the side of your bed. When attached to the side of your bed, one of the side panels is removed. The idea is that a co-sleeper is a good middle ground between having the baby sleep next to you, whilst actually being safe and snug in its own bed.

Cot? Crib? Cradle? Moses basket? Co-sleeper? The options are mind-boggling!

Travel cot: Sleeping suitability varies from model to model. This is similar to a cot, but foldable to make it easier to travel with. A travel cot doesn't have adjustable height and is much less sturdy than a cot.

Whichever bed option you choose, check that it has passed the latest safety regulations – (currently British Standard mark BS EN 716-1).

TRAVELLING TO AWAY GAMES

☑ 1 changing bag
☑ 1 car seat
☑ 1 pushchair

See Chapter 6 - Travel and Away Games for loads of info on these 3 things and more.

CHOOSING WHETHER OR NOT TO USE A DUMMY?

Whether or not you decide to give a dummy (pacifier or soother) to your baby is a matter of personal choice. There's no right or wrong answer. Some parents swear by dummies, and they can help soothe a crying baby. Other parents detest them. If you decide that a dummy is right for you and your baby, then there are a few things to think about:

- If you decide that you want to give

your baby a dummy (and most importantly, if your baby decides that they want to use the dummy) then it's worth buying 4-7 identical dummies, so you always have sterilised ones in reserve and that all lids fit all dummies.

- Sterilise dummies just as you sterilise baby bottles.

- Consider tapering how often you give your baby a dummy, so that your baby doesn't come to rely on the dummy throughout the day. If you want the dummy to be effective at relaxing your baby (or sending your baby to sleep) then it isn't wise to let them have the dummy throughout waking hours.

- Latex, Silicone or Orthodontic? Latex and rubber dummies are meant to be softer and more flexible than silicone dummies but they don't last as long. Silicone dummies are potentially more hygienic. Orthodontic dummies are the third option and are shaped to encourage a baby to suck in a similar way to when they're being breastfed. Orthodontic dummies are also meant to be less likely to affect tooth development.

GET THE STADIUM READY

You'll never be fully prepped, but here are a few things you can do to get ready for the big arrival. Other Dad FC managers have said these become invaluable time-savers after their babies were born:

FREEZE MEALS IN PREPARATION

As my wife entered the early stages of labour, one of the first things I did after rushing home was start making spaghetti Bolognese. Doing this wasn't planned, so it must have been some subconscious paternal instinct kicking in. This Bolognese proved invaluable as we went to and from the hospital over the course of a few days and had no time for cooking. The pot of Bolognese was huge and covered several meals. I like to think of myself as a modern day hunter-gatherer.

ADOPT A HIGH STANDARD OF CLEANING AND STERILISE STUFF

It goes without saying that babies need to grow up in a clean environment and this is extra important when babies are in their first year, when they're most susceptible to common bugs, viruses and colds. If you're used to living in squalor: firstly, well done for finding a partner who can accommodate you and secondly, if there was ever a time to clean up your act, then that time is now. So wash the walls down, clean and polish the furniture and scrub the crusty bogies off the heater next to the sofa.

DRAFT A CLEANER INTO THE CLUB

This one is a matter of choice. We've heard of people investing in cleaners once they become new parents. Why? The reasons and benefits are actually quite clear:

- You get your house cleaned (obviously)

- You don't have to think about the big jobs that eat up your time (when you won't have any time)

- Dull chores such as vacuuming, dusting (who does that?), cleaning the bathroom and even laundry can be covered

- You spend your precious time caring for your baby rather than juggling household work at the same time

Some new parents say that getting a cleaner in, just made sense. Cleaners cost around £10-£15 an hour and there are services available where you get the same cleaner each time, with no contracts and with options on how often the cleaner comes (weekly or fortnightly for example). If you're trying to work out if this is for you, then it helps to put a price on the value of your time.

Some parents make the decision on whether to get a cleaner (or not), like this:

"I make more than £10 an hour (let's say £15 an hour take-home pay for example). I've effectively decided to work for £15 an hour. I don't want to spend an hour at home doing chores that can be done for less money than I'm working for (i.e. chores can be done for £10 an hour and I'm earning £15 an hour). I am saving money every month so I can afford to pay £50 a month."

THE EQUATION THEN BECOMES SIMPLE

£50 a month (which I can afford to live without) v 5 hours a month with my family instead of doing chores I don't want to do.

Or, an alternative way of looking at it: is there something I'd prefer spending the £50 a month on? £50 is £600 a year. This could go towards Christmas, holidays, education or health insurance for example. There are also some potential negatives about having a cleaner:

- Cleaners cost money and your baby has just taken a huge wad of cash out of your monthly pay check

- It takes time to find a cleaner (although it is pretty easy to find them online)

- You may question a cleaner's quality of cleaning versus doing it yourself (How long do they take to clean? Do they clean well?)

- You have to trust giving a stranger access to your home

- You have to be at home, waiting for the cleaner to arrive (it's another date in the calendar and restricts you from doing something else at that time)

- For some people, having a cleaner just feels uncomfortable

So I hope that helps you make the decision. Whilst we personally chose not to get a cleaner, we can see why others might.

PRACTICE YOUR SET PIECES

This one goes without saying. Just how Ronaldo, Rooney and Beckham would stay behind after training to practice their free kicks and corners, new dads should do the same for car seats, bottle feeding and bathing. It's worth grabbing that over-sized teddy that your friend gave you as a baby-shower gift and using it to practice your techniques for giving a baby a bottle, getting a baby into and out of a car seat and bathing too.

See Chapter 3 – Making your Debut for the core set pieces.

FROM THE TERRACES

"What does it feel like to become a dad?"

There's too much pressure put on new parents to feel something special when their baby is born. I've heard many a dad say that "it's the best thing in the world, and when I saw my baby for the first time, I just thought 'I'm gonna protect you forever my little angel' and my heart melted.". I, on the other hand, was more "OK, we are both physically and mentally knackered and I'm just glad everyone's alive. Now... you're really expecting me to look after you?" and I kind of felt like I was faking being a dad at first. You know, you nervously pick the little baby up, without feeling a special bond and you're just scared that it might attack you or start screaming its little lungs out. It was a scary time, but you do get some kind of competence kick in. You've probably done at least some planning for this moment, and whilst your planning will never give you all the preparation needed to be a dad (nothing ever can, not even this here book) you manage to get through the basics OK and find a role for yourself.

So in short, becoming a parent can be an incredible moment, but give yourself a break if it doesn't feel so great when you and your partner are both exhausted and have just been handed the biggest responsibility in the world.

POST-MATCH INTERVIEW:

"I'd completely lost her"

We'd just moved into a house that needed to be completely renovated and we fell pregnant as soon as we started trying (oh yea, that's me...). After feeling quite proud of myself on the one hand, the reality of preparing for becoming a dad was made extra tricky by having to deal with renovating our first property before the little one arrived. There's nothing quite like the arrival of a baby to add pressure to a task. 4 years later and the house renovations are not finished (and probably never will be), but we have a happy and healthy toddler.

I'll admit that I don't like to try loads of new things – this includes playing new sports like skiing or ice skating, making new friends (I'm more of an 'alright once you get to know him' kind of person) or learning a new language. So the feeling of being incompetent can freak me out, so I try to avoid it altogether. Upon becoming a father for the first time, I was filled with a sense of dread that I'd not be up to the job. Being a parent was a completely new experience and like nothing I'd done before.

This feeling of incompetence was backed up before fatherhood, when I asked a sales assistant in Mothercare if it's OK to fold-up a pram whilst the baby is still in it (in my defence I still think that would be excellent product innovation).

Later on, in my first week as a parent: taking our baby out of the house, I tipped the pram forwards and our tiny baby slid from the top to the bottom of the pram — I'd completely lost her in amongst the blankets.

The truth is, in the same way that no one is born walking or talking - no one is born knowing how to look after a child. It's a learned experience. But I do suggest you do a few training drills before the big day!

03. MAKING YOUR DEBUT

"Mistakes will be made, make no mistake"

Garth Crooks

So it's debut day for both you and your new star striker (aka: your baby). The fans have been waiting with much anticipation outside the stadium, granddad is like one of those incredibly annoying photographers, keen to get a snap as soon as the baby mildly changes expression or position, and the new grandmum's are muscling their way into the limelight, like two schoolchildren desperate for an autograph. There's no need to remind you that you're not the biggest new arrival at the club. The star striker is who everyone has come to see and he'll rightly be grabbing all the headlines in these first few days, as fans and pundits wait with bated breath to catch a glimpse of their new starlet.

As manager, the job is to make sure your new arrival settles in well at the club and he is protected from the spotlight he'll come under. New grandparents, uncles, aunts, friends and family will all adore him and you can't blame them. As long as your little one is content at being passed from pillar to post and you have all the basics covered, then you can't keep him under wraps any longer. Here's what you need to know when it comes to keeping the basics covered.

WHAT TO THINK ABOUT ONCE YOUR BABY IS BORN

Like some footballers, your baby will have an insatiable need for attention, a total lack of regard for the worth of money and will not know right from wrong.

It's your duty to work out why he's craving attention, afford the things he needs and keep him out of harm's way. Much of your work falls into 3 categories: feeding, winding and cleaning. There are some other basic set pieces you'll get to grips with too:

SET PIECE 1 – THE BEST WAYS TO HOLD A NEWBORN BABY

One of the first things you'll do with your little one is pick them up. The first time you do this can be both an amazing and apprehensive moment. Amazing because it's the first time you get to say hello to your child; an incredible experience and one that you'll remember forever. Apprehensive because you're afraid that you might just break this fragile little fella. Here's a quick idea of the different ways you can hold your baby.

Some of these will feel more comfortable for you, some will feel more comfortable for the baby. The important thing is to try a few things and you'll soon both get familiar with these and they'll become really enjoyable moments of bonding.

The key thing to remember is to get comfortable and support the baby's head into your arm or body.

1. **Cradle celebration (cradle in your arms):** the first time you'll hold your baby will probably be to cradle him in your arms, when you're sitting down. The baby can be supported across the length of your arm and the baby's head is in the inside of your elbow

2. **Lapping it up (sit in your lap):** put your baby onto your lap with his feet tucked into your tummy, and support his head with your hands

3. **Up against it (up against your chest):** put your baby's bottom into your hand and use your other hand on across shoulders to stop his head from moving around

4. **Going down (lying across your forearm):** cross your forearm and put his head up near your elbow. Your baby's feet should be on either side of your hand. Grip around one leg and you can softly rub your baby's back with the spare hand. This one is great for winding!

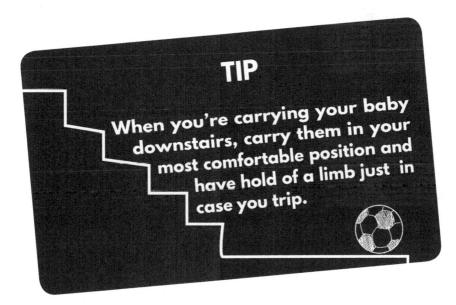

TIP

When you're carrying your baby downstairs, carry them in your most comfortable position and have hold of a limb just in case you trip.

FOLLOW YOUR GUT INSTINCT

You know those moments on the pitch? Those moments when you're not self-conscious and the ball feels as if it's a magnet to your feet? Follow that same instinct when it comes to your baby. You might not always feel this instinct, but when you do, you're probably right.

FIRST DECISION: VITAMIN K AND THE MEDICAL

Possibly the first decision you'll have to make as a new dad is whether or not to give your baby vitamin K and how you want it administered to your baby. Vitamin K helps blood to clot and prevents excessive internal bleeding (which can be caused by a lack of vitamin K). Some newborn babies are at risk of having low levels of vitamin K in their blood, so the Department of Health recommends that all babies are given vitamin K. Most parents accept their babies to have it, often by injection but sometimes by oral supplements. The choice is yours.

Your midwife will also give your newborn a medical; checking things like eyes, heart, hips and testicles. Shortly after this, your baby will then be offered a blood spot test (otherwise known as a heel prick test) to check for rare but serious diseases, and a hearing test to screen for any permanent hearing loss.

WHAT WILL MY BABY LOOK LIKE?

"Judging by the shape of his face, he must have headed a lot of goals"

Harry Redknapp on Iain Dowie

Most people envisage that their baby will look similar to them or their partner. In reality, a newborn baby won't look like either you and will barely look human. If you think your newborn baby might look like smaller, big-headed chubby version of yourself then you're totally mistaken. If you think they'll look like a cross-between Benjamin Button and a battered and bruised Iain Dowie, then you're more on the money.

YOU'LL GET A LITTLE RED BOOK ABOUT YOUR BABY'S HEALTH

Just before or after your child is born you'll be given a PCHR (Personal Child Health Record) which is to keep track of your baby's weight, height, general health and wellbeing as well as any vaccinations and important health info. Your baby will have a few health check-ups and reviews in their first year (usually at a GP or a health clinic) and this is just to ensure that things are all developing as they should. These meetings are a good opportunity for you to ask any questions about your baby's development, progress and any concerns you might have. Don't be afraid to ask anything here – there aren't any stupid questions. Well... there are stupid questions but it's good to get comfortable asking these, so you get 'in the know'.

SET PIECE 2 – DRIVING YOUR BABY HOME

Before you get your baby home, you'll need to embark on what seems like the longest and most troublesome car journey of all time. This fragile little life, which is your responsibility, needs to be transported safely from the hospital to the home. Once home, you need never leave the house again. But first, we'll talk about how you get there.

1. Remember the car seat (as prepared in chapter 2).

2. Strap the car seat in place. The best way for a newborn baby to travel is in a rear-facing (so the baby is facing the opposite way to the way you drive!) infant car seat that goes in the back seat of your vehicle. This car seat can also go in the front passenger seat so long as the front passenger seat is not fitted with an airbag. Whether in the front or

back of the car, the car seat is strapped in place by the adult safety belt in the car.

3. Clothing and temperature. Your baby should feel safe and snug. The general rule of thumb is that your baby should wear one more layer than you. You baby shouldn't feel hot to the touch. Other signs that they're too hot include sweating or damp hair. The temperature in the car should be comfortable for an adult.

4. Strap your baby in and carefully tug the car seat and straps to ensure they're in correctly.

5. Drive away as you normally would - carefully and confidently.

WHAT TO THINK ABOUT AT HOME

BEFORE THE FIRST BOTTLE FEED – STERILISE EVERYTHING

This is a big lesson to learn. The house will get messy, and you have to accept that. However, you can make your new daily life a hell of a lot easier if you look after each room, tend to the washing up and plan the key set pieces beforehand. It's hell on earth when you have a screaming hungry baby and no sterilised bottles to feed the grizzly monster.

STERILISING KIT

There are germs everywhere and you won't be able to get rid of them all. However there are some fundamental things you should do and one of those is sterilising the feeding equipment (and dummies if you use them). Sterilising gets rid of potentially harmful bacteria, viruses and parasites that can make your baby ill. Don't try to be a rogue dad who thinks that 'whatever doesn't kill you makes you stronger' – that's one of those ridiculous sayings and you should be sent from the dugout immediately if you start taking liberties like that.

There are 3 different types of sterilising: cold water sterilising, boiling water sterilising and steam sterilising. Whichever you choose, you need to wash all bottle parts and teats in warm soapy water before sterilising.

1. **Cold water sterilising:** these sterilising sets can be bought in many pharmacies and baby stores. Simply follow the instruction manual that comes with the equipment, which usually requires you to fill the cold water steriliser with the washed-up bottles and include a sterilising fluid. These machines tend to take around 15-20 minutes to sterilise completely and the bottles are often then ready-to-use straight away. Again, read those instructions to ensure you get it right.

2. **Boiling water sterilising** is when you put the bottle parts in boiling hot water for 10 minutes to kill the germs. Avoid the schoolboy error of boiling something that isn't meant to be boiled (check instruction manuals if you're unsure). Teats are more delicate that the actual bottles so check them for damage and replace them if you find tears.

Wash your hands before touching the sterilised items and always be careful with hot pans. Once boiled, if you're not using the parts immediately then put the parts together to prevent the inside of the bottle getting contaminated. If you're using the bottle right away, just ensure the bottle has cooled down before you begin the feed.

3. **Steam sterilising** is when there's an electrical steriliser that kills the germs via steaming them to death. A little tip here is to place the openings of bottles, teats and lids face-down in the steriliser. This stops the condensed water from sitting in them. As with the cold water steriliser, read the instruction manual to know exactly how long it takes to sterilise and for how long you can leave a sterilised bottle unused before needing to sterilise it again.

TRICKS AND TIPS: SHOWBOAT

You're going to need bottles, food pots and (depending on your preference) dummies (or soother, pacifier, whatever). Buy lots of the same model. Don't buy a few different brands or different models of bottles, for example. You want to be able to grab a bottle, bottle lid and teat, and KNOW that they will all fit together. You won't want to spend time messing around looking for the right sized teat when you've got a demanding baby in your midst. Dummies come with their own plastic holder, so again, you want to be able to grab any holder and know it'll fit the dummy.

SET PIECE 3 – BOTTLE FEEDING

"Feed the Goat and he will score!"
Manchester City fans chant for
Ex-Manchester City striker Shaun Goater

You can't breastfeed, but you *can* help when it comes to feeding time. Making up a bottle is pretty simple and there are some basic things to bear in mind. Here are some steps I used when making a formula bottle.

1. Sterilise everything (bottle, teat, lid)

2. Boil water, let it cool to c.70 degrees (which is still very hot and hot enough to kill any bacteria) and add water to bottle

3. Add formula powder to bottle – always read the instructions on the back of the pack to ensure you get the proportions correct

4. Put the teat on then twist the cap on

5. Shake it up, test the temperature is warm by splashing a little on your wrist

6. Too hot? Put a lid on and rinse under the cold tap until it's warm

7. Serve, tilting the bottle as you go, to ensure that the end of the teat is full of milk and your little one doesn't end up consuming air (which would later cause wind and discomfort)

Foul!
Don't store and reheat previous feeds!

THE BREAST MILK EXPRESS

"All aboard! Tickets please!" Dads can hop onto this ride too. If your partner is expressing breast-milk then it can be stored in the fridge and keeps for up to 5 days if your fridge is cooler than 4°C. There's no medical study to say that your baby has to have the milk warmed up, but as breast milk is naturally expressed at a warm temperature, your little one may find it more comforting to enjoy a warm bottle, so just heat up the bottle in a pan of boiled water.

Dry the bottle then test the temperature by dribbling a bit of the breast milk onto your wrist. This might feel a bit weird at first, having come from your partner and all, but you'll stop caring about these small things within a couple of days. Oh, and breast milk can also be frozen (for up to 6 months!) and defrosted in the fridge. Once defrosted, use the milk within 1 hour and bin anything you don't use.

TRICKS AND TIPS

- Don't store and reheat previous feeds
- Never refreeze breast milk once it's thawed
- Never microwave milk as it can cause hotspots which can burn
- Always use sterilised containers

SET PIECE 4 – WINDING

After a feed, it's a good habit to give your little one a gentle pat on the back for a job well done. This pat on the back also serves as a great way to get the wind out of them. Babies can devour milk at incredible speeds and this can make them need a hefty (or not so hefty) burp. Hold your baby upright, perhaps over your shoulder and rub or pat them on the back (put a muslin cloth over your shoulder to avoid getting covered in any regurgitated milk that might come your way). Check if your little one wants more food – they might have just needed to have a little break to get rid of any gas.

Reflux: reflux in babies is common and it's when your baby brings up milk from a recent feed. It can freak you out a little when you see it for the first time, but it's perfectly natural and happens throughout the first year for many babies. Try to be chilled out if and when it happens. You could try burping your baby at regular intervals during feeds and also sit them upright after the feed so that the milk flows down to their tummies a little easier. If you're concerned that it's happening too often then it is worth checking the size of the hole in the teat isn't too large, and that your baby isn't consuming too much milk in one sitting. Basically, don't force the little one to have more food than he wants. He might prefer more frequent smaller feeds than a big gorge.

TIP

Teat's do have different sized holes, so as your baby gets older, upsize the teat so that they can get more milk out with each suck. A sign that you need to go up to the next sized teat (or 'flow stage') is when the teat is collapsing in on itself during the feed.

SET PIECE 5 – CHANGING NAPPIES – TACKLING DIRTY

One of the things that some new dads find surprising is that cleaning dirty bottoms isn't as bad as they thought it might be. For a few, the mere whiff of a soiled nappy is enough to make them wretch and make for the exit. Dad F.C. is keen for these managers to man-up and get involved here. You're going to need to become acquainted with dirty nappies and like anything, practice makes perfect.

How often your little one needs to be changed depends on a number of things, including their age, what they're consuming and how sensitive their skin is. In the early days, it's usual to change the nappy up to about 10-12 times a day. A soiled nappy should be changed immediately or as soon as possible to avoid both discomfort and nappy rash. A wet nappy could be changed immediately or you could wait until before or after a feed (whichever seems right for your baby – as long as they're comfortable and not getting a rash).

KIT BAG

Like bath time, it's massively important to get the groundsman in and get the place tidy and prepared before you begin.
PS – you are the groundsman.

☑ Changing mat
☑ Towel (as a spare or in place of the changing mat)
☑ Fresh nappy

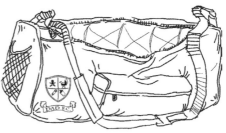

☑ Cotton wool
☑ Warm water
☑ Baby wipes (sensitive non-alcohol type are best)
☑ Nappy sack (for the dirty nappy and dirty cotton wool)
☑ Cream (nappy rash cream for keeping baby's bum protected)
☑ Clean clothes

EXTRA KIT WORTH CONSIDERING

☑ A nappy holder (for storing all the fresh nappies nearby)
☑ A baby changing table or a cot-top changer (this can avoid back pain but keep your eye on your baby at all times as they have an incredible knack of doing their first roll at just the wrong time)
☑ Dirty laundry basket nearby (you'll be emptying this basket regularly, but it helps to have a laundry basket nearby so you can throw dirty clothes straight into it, before taking it all to the washing machine)
☑ Cleaning spay: to wash the changing mat clean after use. Use a baby wipe to wipe clean.

1. Wash your hands.

2. Lay the little one down on the mat, remove their clothes (or lift the clothes up if the clothes are not dirty and don't need to be changed) and open the nappy

3. Lift the baby's legs up by using one hand to lift up at ankles.

4. If the baby has done a number 2 (poo) then use the nappy to wipe as much of the poo into the nappy. Close the dirty

nappy and keep it under the baby's bum to avoid the baby's dirty bum touching the changing mat.

5. Grab a piece of cotton wool, dab it in the warm water and clean the rest of the poo off the baby's skin. If your baby has just done a number 1 (wee) then you still give your baby the same good clean, always being careful to wipe between the folds of their chubby legs.

6. Once fully cleaned, remove the dirty nappy from beneath the baby and place the dirty nappy and the used cotton wool balls inside a nappy bag.

7. Have a good chat with your baby when you're doing this. This is a decent time to bond, so pull faces and have a giggle. You want to make sure your baby has a healthy relationship with going to the toilet and doesn't get any negative vibes about doing a number 1 or 2.

8. Grab a fresh nappy, open it and place it, open side up, under your baby.

9. Let go of his little ankles and bring the front side of the nappy up, so it sits comfortably around his belly. For a boy, make sure his penis is down, rather than up – otherwise next time he goes for a wee you'll all get covered.

10. Bring the left and right folds over, sticking them snugly (not tightly) onto the front of the nappy. If your baby still has an umbilical cord stump then roll the front of the nappy so that the cord is not touching nor covered by the nappy.

SHOWBOAT

Most baby onesies and vests are designed with shoulder flaps. You can flick these shoulder flaps inside out, bringing your baby's arms up comfortably through the neck of the vest, and pull or roll the onesie down over their legs rather than over their head. Why do you care? Because this avoids getting dirt all up your baby's back if you were to pull a dirty onesie over their head.

SET PIECE 6 – BATHING – HITTING THE SHOWERS

This can be daunting at first, but you can make this into a really fun and enjoyable time for the family. Yes, the little one may or may not like the first few baths, but the way you behave and how chilled out you are can really make a difference to how well your baby takes to bath time.

Practice the skills of putting the baby in the bath, bathing them, washing the umbilical cord, taking the baby out the bath (seriously, do this with a doll if it helps) and 2 things will happen as a result:

1) you'll begin to memorise the actions which helps you bathe your baby more confidently, and

2) towels, sponge, soap, bath thermometer, you name it, are all exactly where you need them as you'll have started a routine.

Both these 2 benefits will create a much more enjoyable experience for both dad and baby.

KIT BAG

☑ Bath tub
☑ 2 towels
☑ Cotton wool
☑ Fresh nappy
☑ Clean clothes
☑ Nappy sack for old nappy
☑ Nappy rash cream (to hand if required)
☑ Warm water (37 °C)

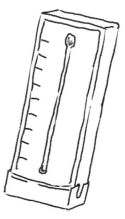

THE BATH-TIME

1. Fill the bath with cold water first, then hot water. Get it to 8-10 cm and check the temperature using the thermometer or your elbow – you're looking for the bath to be at body temperature, which is about 37 °C. No bath liquids are required, just water will do perfectly for at least the first 5 weeks.

2. Undress your baby down to a vest and keep him warm in a towel. Gently wash his face, eyes, ears, neck, hands, and then genitals using cotton wool pads or cotton wool balls tabbed in the warm water. Use separate bits of cotton wool for different areas to avoid infections.

3. Remove the vest and carefully lift your baby out of the towel and support him with one of your arms under his bottom and your

other arm reaching around the back of his shoulders – supporting his neck and head. Hold onto your baby's arm which is furthest away from you.

4. Wash your baby's hair with plain water then dry their head.

5. Keep your baby's head up and clear of the water and use your other hand (the one that was supporting his bottom) to gently wash your baby's body with the warm water. You can use a soft sponge if you like.

6. Lift your baby out of the water and gently dry them completely, especially making sure you get those cute chubby folds and creases in their skin completely dry.

RED CARD

NEVER LEAVE A BABY OR CHILD UNDER 5 ALONE IN THE BATH, NOT EVEN FOR ½ A SECOND

TRICKS AND TIPS: PAMPER

It's well known that footballers are very pampered these days. Some managers now give their star strikers massages after bath. This helps the player relax before bed and creates a bond between manager and player. You could do the same with your baby.

UMBILICAL CORD

The remaining 2-3cm of umbilical cord (or 'eeuurrgggghhh' as it is affectionately known due to its rather unpleasant shrivelled appearance), will remain on your baby for about 5-15 days after birth. Keep this clean and dry and let it come off on its own – don't pull at it. You might prefer to just give your baby a top and tail wash instead of a bath whilst the stump is still on – whatever you feel comfortable with. To prevent infection, gently clean the stump with warm water on a cotton wool ball when you're doing nappy changes. You'll know if it's infected because it'll start weeping or become red or swollen. If it does become red or swollen then consult your midwife or doctor.

CUTTING NAILS

Babies can have really long, razor sharp nails – which they can inadvertently scratch themselves (or even worse, you!) with their mini Scissorhands. When they go to sleep at night you can put on these cute little mittens (no, not on you, silly! On the baby!) to make sure there are no self-inflicted injuries. Perhaps better still, you could cut the nails with special baby rounded-ended nail scissors, or use a fine emery board nail file. How sweet.

FROM THE TERRACES

"When should I give my baby his first bath?"

Great question. Again, there's no exact answer. Newborn babies have a white moisture on them, called Vernix. This natural moisture helps the baby build up a skin barrier and also cleanses the skin. Due to these benefits, it's normal to hear of parents waiting at a few days or a week before giving their baby its first bath. In the meantime, just a 'top and tail' (step 2 of bath-time) is sufficient. If your baby and you love bath-time, then there's no reason why you can't start bathing earlier. Some people give their babies a bath within a few hours of being born, some wait a week before giving their baby its first bath.

"How many times a week should I bathe my baby?"

There's no one answer to this, but around 2-3 times a week is normal, but if you want to do it every day then that's all good if the baby is happy and this helps you get a routine going.

CRYING

All ~~footballers~~ babies cry, and it's something you'll get used to. You'll also get used to the different cries that your baby makes and you will start to understand what your little one is trying to tell you with each cry.

Fundamentally it comes down to your baby wanting some kind of comfort or care, and this will usually be that your baby needs to be fed, changed or winded. He may even just want to be cuddled and close to you or his mum. How cute.

MOST COMMON REASONS YOUR BABY MIGHT BE CRYING

- Hungry
- Tired
- Dirty nappy
- Too hot or too cold
- Illness
- Comfort (including where they're sitting, bright lights, noise)
- Needs winding
- Wants a cuddle

THINGS TO HELP YOUR BABY STOP CRYING

Naturally, there are some basic things on here for you to do, and we've covered the likes of feeding, winding / burping your baby, tiredness and changing a nappy. Use your common sense when it comes to changing the temperature, clothing or environment your little one is in. Ask yourself the question: how would I feel in this room if I was new to the world? That bright light that's always on in the corner of the room, or Martin Tyler's voice booming out of the 42" TV can be offensive to many-an-ear. Think about toning down things that affect your baby's senses: smell, sight, touch and sound.

However, there are some occasions when your baby just seems to cry for no reason. You've gone through the list, you know they're not hungry and their nappy is completely clean. You've even checked their temperature to be sure there's nothing up. Here are a few things you could try:

- A dummy or muslin cloth as a comforter
- A dummy (sterilised just the same as a bottle)
- Use a co-sleeper at bedtime so that they can feel your closeness
- Try swaddling
- Softly sing and gently rock your baby from side to side
- Gently rub your baby's back and keep talking softly to them – your voice can be comforting
- Distract your baby with new stimuli, like music or a mobile above their cot

Babies can pick up on your anxiety, so try to stay calm for both you and your baby's benefit. Asking an experienced family member, such as your own parents, or a close friend who has raised children of their own can help, as people have picked up their own tips and tricks on the way. You can also speak to your health visitor or midwife if you have concerns or are struggling with crying.

MEETING THE FANS AND PRESS

Mass hysteria is part and parcel of every big arrival at Dad FC. Fans will want to drop in and the press will want to ask questions. Whilst most visitors are welcome, there can be the occasional time when you'd rather play behind closed doors. Here's a Who's Who? of visitors in your first few weeks of fatherhood.

PUNDITS

You might feel that these guys are judging you, or even worse, your baby. That's because they probably are. They'll over analyse how sensitive your partner is, how the mess in the kitchen sink is a sign you're not coping as a new manager, and that you don't seem to be gelling with your baby. You know what? You won't care about any of this, and shouldn't. They'll be so insignificant in comparison to your new job and what's important in your life right now. The best thing you can do is ignore it all and focus on today.

GLORY SUPPORTERS

These guys don't seem to really care much, but just know that this is where the action is right now. They'll take a few photos, or not, and won't really care to make themselves useful for you. Like most glory supporters, these fans turn into armchair fans pretty quickly; liking the odd baby photo on social media but probably won't bother visiting you or inviting you to theirs anytime soon. They're just not into babies, and that's fine – your baby didn't seem much into them either.

DIE-HARD FANS

These guys are there for you through thick and thin. You don't even need to ask and they'll just be there to help. Whether it's washing up, telling you about their parental experiences and sharing their own wisdom, or just listening and supporting what you're going through – you'll never take their loyalty for granted.

POLICE PRESENCE AT TODAY'S GAME

A small word of warning – set boundaries with fans. Make sure visiting times are controlled by you and your partner's schedule, not by theirs. Be consistent on how you expect them to behave - most fans have some level of common sense, but there are the odd few who'll stick an unwashed finger into your baby's mouth, or dangle your 2-week-old upside down.

Set the record straight and lead by example. Don't be afraid to ask people to wash their filthy adult hands, not puff cigarette smoke into your baby's face or chant racist, homophobic or in any way offensive songs, no matter how much they nervously laugh "Look! He likes it! He likes it!" And don't worry about "postponing" tomorrow's fixture.

FROM THE TERRACES

"How soon should we have visitors round? When should we invite the family round?"

With all of these things, there isn't one answer. We're all human beings and therefore all do things differently. Some of your family will want to come round on the first day or before, and will be chomping at the bit to see you and your new family. That's great, so long as you and your partner are happy to have them.

Most family members just want to help out, and this help can be much-needed in the first few weeks. Other family or friends may respectfully keep a distance in the early days, so as not to get in the way. They know you've got enough to deal with.

Get used to asking friends and family when you're ready for a visit and when you need any help. Having a new grandparent around can really take the strain off things, and give you time for a shower, shave or sleep. Grandparents have 'been there and done that', so can help with either looking after the baby or doing some housework. Ask them to help in the ways you want them to help. It's worth being clear with them from the outset — you are in charge and that they can't just take responsibilities from you, whether that's taking the baby for a feed, or tidying your partner's lingerie drawer.

POST-MATCH INTERVIEW:

So the big day has been and gone. I thought it was time to give myself a big pat on the back. I'd got through the birth and that did not go as smoothly as we'd laid out in the birthing plan. What happened to the natural, unassisted birth, with calming classical music seeing us through the best day or night of our lives?

I felt guilty for actually thinking about myself, but it isn't easy seeing your loved one go through labour for four days solid and not being able to do anything about it. Seriously, four days and nights of hospital visits, the baby seems to progress with the dilation, then retreats back up and closes the door behind him! Then it all ended quite unpleasantly, but the less said about that the better.

Every couple's experience of labour will be different – but I certainly felt more of a sense of relief than actual celebration when our daughter was born. Relief that my wife was alive, albeit zombified, and that the new arrival was present and well too. The birth took so long that we had to give up our 2012 Olympics ticket – I didn't resent the little scamp one bit.

The following 7 days was really up and down. In some ways, anything went: take a shower, don't take a shower. Eat, don't eat. Sleep, definitely don't sleep. The fact that both parents are physically and mentally spent after the labour, only to have to start with the job of being new parents, is a big kick-in-the-balls. However, you've got to give yourself a dressing down pretty quick and pick yourself back up and get on with your new role at Dad F.C.

It was great to have the grandparents around for the first couple of nights; we only wish it was longer, as we were a bit all over the place at first. Our daughter was causing mayhem with the breast (both nipples were practically dangling off!) and there was no sign of a routine. Having someone just help with the normal house work and then lend a helpful ear when it came to giving our baby her first bath was invaluable. I was still nervous giving the bath but having my mum's support really helped.

Your role as manager of Dad FC starts now. There will be trials and tribulations, but now is the time when you can really start to get involved and make a difference to the life of your baby. Here are some key pointers that will help you through the first few weeks.

04. SLEEP AND 3AM KICK OFFS

"Football is like fighting a gorilla – you don't stop when you're tired, you can only stop when the gorilla is tired"

Chris Coleman

And the shrill of the ref's whistle blew to signal the end of 90 minutes. Extra time had been on the cards since half time. It'd been a long and hard fought game, with dirty nappies, a couple of teething red cheeks and a biting incident which left a sour taste in the mouth.

Bedtime can be one of the best parts of being a dad. Spending some quality time with your baby at the end of the day is not only a great way to finish a busy day but also gives you and your baby time to bond. Getting into a routine after a few weeks or months is really helpful for making bedtime as smooth and relaxing as possible. So draw back the curtains, put the soft light on and settle down for a short bedtime story before a long winter's nap.

Are you sitting comfortably? Then I shall begin...

PUTTING THE BABY INTO BED

The set piece here is easy to learn, but difficult to master. Follow the basic instructions but, as with all of these set pieces, use your common sense.

SAFETY FIRST

Before you lay the little one down for their first sleeps, check that the mattress fits snugly with no space where your baby's head or limbs may get stuck. Any bars on the cot or crib should be completely smooth, secure and have no less than 25mm and no more than 60mm between each bar. The cot itself needs to be strong and sturdy, with no loose ties or fabrics that your baby could get tangled in.

HOW TO LAY THEM DOWN

It's recommended by health professionals that you lay your baby down in a "feet-to-foot" position, which means that your baby's feet are at the end (or 'foot') of the bed when they go down to sleep. This reduces the risk of covers coming up onto your baby's face as your baby moves in the night. You should also lay your baby on their back (not on their front or side).

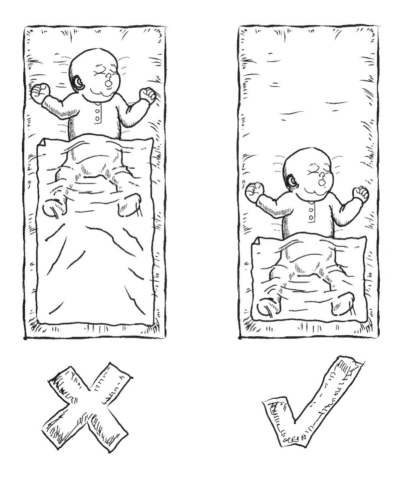

Lay your little one down so that his feet are at the foot of the bed.

WHAT A BABY SHOULD WEAR IN BED

- If it's an ideal temperature of around 18-19 degrees then a 2.5 tog sleeping bag plus a long-sleeved bodysuit Dress your baby in comfortable clothes. As a rule of thumb, babies should wear one more layer than you would.

- Try to use 100% cotton clothing as this is more breathable on their skin.

- Never put a hat on your baby when they're going to sleep.

- You could add mittens to your baby's hands if they have sharp nails (to stop them scratching themselves in the night)

A ROUGH IDEA OF HOW THEY MIGHT SLEEP AS THEY GROW

Newborn: 8-18 hours sleep. He will sleep often and maybe sleep more than he's awake. Expect to be woken up in the night by the baby needing food or possibly being too hot or cold. After a few weeks could start to introduce the concept of night and day but don't expect any kind of routine until about 8 weeks.

3-6 months: He'll start to sleep more in the night (maybe up to 8 hours) than in the day and take fewer night feeds. This process can be helped by the routine you put in place.

6-12 months: He may now sleep through the night, but don't be surprised if this isn't the case. Teething could also cause discomfort and begin to wake them. They could now sleep for around 12-15 hours and still get one or two naps during the day.

SLEEP ROUTINES

Many parents talk of trying to establish routines, especially around their baby's sleeping patterns. Newborn babies tend to sleep sporadically throughout the day, in short naps, with feeds in between. In the first 24-48 hours your baby may sleep most of the time – mum isn't the only one who's just gone through labour! Some babies will then start sleeping up to 18 hours a day in total, whilst others can be sleeping much less than that, at around 8 hours.

Some babies will have short naps whilst others will sleep until the cows come home. The point is, every baby is different so you don't need to worry if you know of a friend's baby who is sleeping much more or less than yours.

You could try to get a routine when they're about 8-12 weeks old, but don't worry if it's not completely working. Keep trying but don't fret about it as it can take time. Once you think you've nailed it, you're only 1 week away from it being turned upside down and you've got to start a new routine all over again. Your baby is growing, so there will always be changes to get used to. Here are some things that can help create a relaxing bedtime routine:

EXAMPLE OF AN ENJOYABLE ROUTINE FOR BOTH OF YOU

1. Soft lights come on and curtains close.

2. If you have the TV on, this can go off. Play quiet music and have the bedtime feed.

3. Upstairs for a wash or bath and a baby massage.

4. Into the soothing bedroom and into bedclothes. A quiet bedtime story or soft music.

5. Give them a kiss and cuddle and gently lay them down to fall asleep in their cot or Moses basket.

MAKE THE BABY'S ROOM A THEATRE OF DREAMS

- A mobile, that can play relaxing nursery rhyme sounds
- A soft light in case you need to turn the light on in the middle of the night
- A ticking clock to give the baby a rhythm akin to his mother's beating heart before he was born
- Soft colour tones
- Black out blinds and / or curtains
- If you don't have double glazed windows then now is a great time to get them. This keeps the temperature of the room more consistent and easier to keep warm. It also muffles out any sounds from outdoors.

- A nice temperature – around 18 degrees is ideal, so just adjust the amount of bedding and clothing you use if the temperature is higher or lower.
- 100% cotton bed linen instead of anything polyester. Cotton is more breathable.

Create your own theatre of dreams with a night-light, soft lamp, black out curtains, cotton sheets and a musical mobile.

MAKE YOUR BABY COMFORTABLE

- Your baby shouldn't be hungry, but also shouldn't have literally just eaten. You could try a smaller feed about half an hour before you put your baby down to bed. Nobody likes to go to bed on a full stomach and you wouldn't want build a direct association between feeding and sleeping, otherwise they may want a feed in the middle of the night, in order to be able to go back to sleep.

- Put the little one to bed in a clean nappy. It's best not to put them down immediately after a bath as this could over stimulate them.

- Keep your little one relaxed and in a soothing environment. Don't have loud noises or bright lights around them.

- Don't play with your baby.

CRYING IN THE NIGHT

WHAT'S NORMAL WHEN IT COMES TO CRYING IN THE NIGHT?

All babies cry and no two babies are exactly the same. It's very common for a baby to wake regularly and cry on and off throughout the night for all the common reasons (hungry, dirty, over stimulated, too hot, too cold, too bored – the list goes on). There is no 'normal' when it comes to bedtime and babies crying, so you just have to learn what your little one is trying to tell you and keep calm.

WHAT TO DO WHEN THEY WAKE IN THE NIGHT (WHICH THEY WILL)...

Firstly, so that your baby understands its bedtime and that there's a difference between night and day, there are some tricks and tips worth considering it's helpful to keep things quieter in the house. You and your partner could adopt quieter voices for bedtime, but don't tiptoe around, as your baby should get used to the normal sounds of the house: flushing toilet, people talking and football on TV etc. It's about getting the balance right. You don't want to stimulate your baby before and during the bedtime hours, but you want them to get comfortable with some background noise.

Whatever you do to create a sleep-inducing environment, your baby will probably wake up at some point. Newborns wake up often because they need feeding, but also because they are either too hot or too cold.

- Check the temperature of the room, which should be between 16-20 degrees. A baby monitor with a temperature gauge is a convenient way of checking.
- Check he's clean and hasn't wet the bed. Change his nappy and bed linen if needed.
- If he needs feeding, try to feed him in the bedroom, so he's not changing environment.
- Only turn a soft light on if you need to. Don't turn any bright lights on as this will only further wake up your baby.
- Get both parents to help with the feeds. One can prepare a bottle whilst the other soothes the baby.
- Don't play with them or talk to them as you would during the day. For example, you might blow raspberries on their tummy when changing their nappy during the day as it makes them smile or chuckle - don't do this in evening as it'll only stimulate them and further wake them.

Babies can prefer to just sleep in their mum's or dad's arms and can fall asleep during breastfeeding. They like to be comforted and need the close human contact. So if your little one is restless when they're put down in their Moses basket or cot then that's completely normal. Over time they will (hopefully!) get used to their surroundings but this could take months or even years. We've heard of parents who have waited 3 years for a week without a broken night. Other babies can start to sleep through the night after about 8 weeks!

TACTIC

Use a bedside crib as a safer alternative to bed-sharing

CRYING CONTINUALLY FOR A LONG TIME IS NOT NORMAL

We're not talking about whether or not you should leave your baby to cry (there are conflicting strategies here and it's open to opinion), we're talking about continual crying whilst you are trying to soothe your baby. If you've tried the soothing, feeding, changing and other things and they don't seem to be working, then your baby may have colic (which is essentially a word for intense crying for long periods). Colic is not harmful and isn't your fault – it does mean that your baby will need a lot of winding, rocking, bathing and massages to help soothe them. We cover this in a bit more detail in chapter 9 on first aid and medical. If you have any health concerns, you could speak to a friend, relative, your health visitor or a doctor.

DAD'S SLEEP AND SLEEP DEPRIVATION

Most adults get around 7 ½ - 9 hours sleep a night. When you're a new parent, you'll get around 30 minutes a night.
Just kidding. Some people survive on 6 hours sleep a night, and that's without kids, but most people would feel the effects of just 6 hours.

As a new parent, you'll find there are nights when you get just a few hours sleep, and yes, you can survive this, but there are trade-offs that come in the form of increased levels of stress and anxiety, a lack of focus on tasks, being short-tempered, difficulty remembering things and catching more colds and viruses. It's not going to be easy. The best thing you can do is get as much sleep as you can, when you can. Try to sleep when the baby sleeps in the early days and try to maintain a healthy diet.

If you're not back at work, then it's definitely worth trying to get some sleep during the day when your baby is asleep. This'll help you when it comes to getting up in the middle of the night for feeds.
There's no special secret to it - you'll just have to get used to operating on less sleep. This can make you feel as if you're constantly hung-over and you can lose focus on everyday tasks. So here's a bunch of tried and tested tactics for dealing with lack of sleep when you're back at work:

- Go for a walk
- Exercise at lunch time
- Drink plenty of water
- Eat healthier
- Caffeine pick-me-ups

- The commute: sleep on the train
- Hand over eyes, look down at a sheet of numbers with a pen in your hand, as if you're working
- Sleep in the toilet

WHO DOES THE NIGHT FEEDS?

This can end up being a very hot topic between new parents. Truth be told, when either of you are tired; there's a chance that tensions can run high. The best way to tackle the night time routine is for you both to be clear on what you expect of your partner and yourself. That way, you both know where you stand going into the evening. Even when you do plan things, you might not feel you're always able to deliver on your commitment to get up in the middle of the night. Slip ups are OK, but try to get to know yourself and be accountable for what you say you were going to do. Here are some things that you might want to try. As this is such a hot topic, we have removed the gender of the parents, who are now simply referred to as **At home parent** (AHP) and **Working parent** (WP).

AHP does all nights v WP sleeps

AHP can sleep during the day when the baby sleeps. WP's boss will not allow sleep at work, or WP will soon become an AHP

AHP does working nights v WP does non-working nights

AHP can sleep during the day when baby sleeps. WP can take their turn when not working the next day.

AHP does 02:00-07:00 v WP does 21:00-01:00

Both parents effectively share the load, but the WP gets a solid 5 hours before going to work.

AHP and WP both get up

Both parents get up in the night. Even if the baby needs breast-milk and isn't on an expressed breast milk bottle, WP still get's up for moral support and to help in any way possible.

AHP sleeps v WP does all nights

No. Just, no.

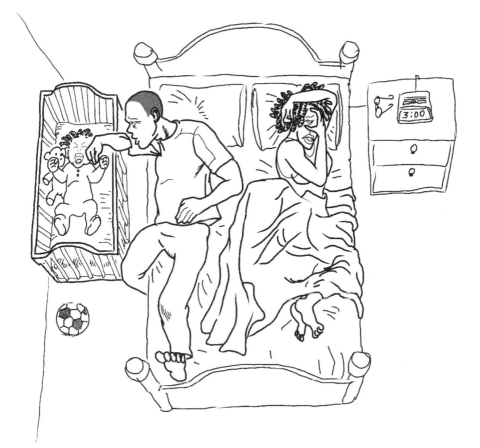

Would you get up in the night if you were working the next morning?

FROM THE TERRACES

"Should I let my baby cry at night"

Once you're 3-6 months into being a new dad, sleep deprivation can really start to take its toll on both parents. This is when some parents start to try sleep training for their baby. There are generally 2 schools of thought on sleep training. One is to let your baby self soothe and the other is to tend to their crying.

If you're taking the self soothe approach, some babies are capable of putting themselves back to sleep from about 3-4 months old. Some parents let their baby cry for a few minutes (some up to 10 minutes maximum), but you should only leave them for how long you feel comfortable with. You could try to gradually increase the time you leave your baby to cry; seeing if they fall asleep after 5 minutes instead of the 3 minutes you previously left them for.

For other parents, leaving a baby to cry just does not feel right. There are ways to tend to your baby's crying whilst encouraging them to sleep more.

If you're taking the approach of tending to their crying, then it's a good idea to gradually soothe them less and less. You're kind of testing their boundaries, giving them shorter and fewer cuddles for example. The idea is to find out how little of you they need. Eventually all you need to do is put your hand on their chest and 'sshhhh' them for 30 seconds.

Try to be consistent (i.e. don't leave her crying for 5 minutes, then the next time she cries go straight in) and give your technique some time to work. Try your method for about 5-7 nights and you could start to see some results. A consistent bedtime routine can really help too.

"When should I put my baby in their own room?"

As a rough rule, parents tend to keep their baby in the same room as them for the first 6 months. After this point, the little ones go into their own bedroom. Whether your baby is sleeping in your room or their own room, it's good to keep the same sleep-inducing conditions.

POST–MATCH INTERVIEW

We'd been struggling with the lack of sleep and lack of routine, and had got into a habit of keeping the little one downstairs with us until about 10pm when we all went upstairs together. The baby generally seemed happy with this too – and I guess it kind of became a routine by default. It all changed one afternoon when our little one was about 13 weeks old. My partner attended one of those weekly baby play groups and, upon eavesdropping on another mum's bragging, she learned that this mum had just started to put her baby to bed, on his own, at around 7pm. And it worked! We tried this, and after about 1 week, our baby daughter got used to this and we slowly started to have a part of our evenings back.

There's no shadow of a doubt that the lack of sleep is a big game-changer when it comes to having kids. The biggest horror story I've heard was a new dad of twins. He, along with his partner, were surviving on a couple of hours sleep here and there, and hadn't had half a night's sleep for months since the birth. When the drained dad went downstairs in the middle of the night to make a formula bottle, he boiled the kettle and took the opportunity to get 2 minutes sleep on the kitchen floor. I suppose a watched kettle never boils.

05. BABY V. FOOD

"I did not see the incident"

Arsene Wenger

OK, OK we hear you. Baby advice circulates much like football gossip. One day you'll be told that formula milk has the full backing of the board, then tomorrow's newspaper reports that formula milk has left the shelves by mutual consent.

MILK

"Daddy, what's the score?! Bottle or Breast, what's the score?!"

Some parents will give their baby both breast and formula milk. Some will give just breast milk and some will give just formula.

BREAST FEEDING AND ITS BENEFITS

The great thing about breast feeding is that it's a great bonding experience between mum and baby. Little ones just love to snuggle up and enjoy a good feed, sometimes falling fast asleep mid-feed, drunk on breast milk. Once a baby has latched on, it's also incredibly convenient for a mum to feed a baby from the breast, as opposed to going through the bottle-making rigmarole required for a formula feed.

One of the biggest benefits of all when it comes to breast feeding is its nutritional value for your baby. Breast milk gives your baby the nutrients it needs and helps build up a stronger immune system. In fact, a mum's breast milk actually adapts as her baby grows, ensuring that the little one has the right nutrients for its age. The benefits are said to last into adulthood too. There are also health benefits for the mum – with breastfeeding helping to reduce the risks of some cancers and diseases. Breast feeding can also help a mum recover from the birth and lose some excess weight she gained through pregnancy.

So that's a thumbs up!

WHAT ARE THE BENEFITS OF BOTTLE FEEDING?

If breast milk is your team captain, who's come through the club's youth academy, then formula milk is the new big-money signing from abroad. It costs you a lot more money and just doesn't deliver the same results.

So feeding your baby formula milk doesn't come with the nutritional advantages of breast feeding and it does cost you more money. So why do people use formula milk and are there any benefits?

Less effort and less pain. Some mothers can struggle with the breast feeding process or simply don't want to breast feed for their own personal reasons. It's quite common for mums to start with just breast feeding and then be concerned that they're not able to give the baby all the food he needs. Being able to grab a formula bottle, or better still, having you there to take the load and get involved in night feeds, means that there is less stress and strain on the mum.

COMBINING BREAST AND BOTTLE MILK

Bottle milk is used by some parents as a sort of 'top-up' if mum has run out of natural supplies. If this happens, it's important that mum doesn't feel like she's been subbed off and replaced by bottle milk, so be supportive and encouraging.

Using formula milk to supplement breast milk could become a vicious circle if it's not monitored. If your baby is having more regular feeds of formula milk, then the baby will not need so much breast milk. As a result, the mum may start to produce less milk. With less breast milk being produced, there's a fair chance you'll use more formula to supplement. And so on and so forth. So if you're keen on breast-feeding, it's wise to consider how much formula milk is being used as the alternative option for feeding your baby.

HOW DO I KNOW IF THEY'VE HAD ENOUGH MILK?

Your baby will be on breast milk (or formula milk) alone from birth to around 4-6 months.

If you (or more specifically your partner) are breastfeeding then your baby will drink a very concentrated type of breast milk called colostrum. As the milk is going straight from the breast to the baby, it can be difficult to tell exactly how much milk they're drinking. Babies only need about a teaspoon full of this stuff when they're first born, and after a couple of days, your partner will begin to produce more and more breast milk.

It's rare for women to not produce enough breast milk for their baby, but good signs that babies are drinking enough milk are that a) they're having their first wet nappies (and soft yellowy stool after 3-5 days), b) they're relaxed during feeds, and c) they are relaxed after feeds.

From after a couple of weeks old they'll need around 150-200ml of milk per kilo of their body weight.

Signs that a baby is hungry include moving around as soon as they wake up, putting their fingers in their mouth and moving their head and mouth around. Crying for food is another sign – and you'll start to identify the particular crying sound so you know that they're ready to eat.

After a week, things usually work themselves out and your partner and baby get into a good flow. After a feed your baby will probably appear very chilled out and relaxed – similar to yourself after a few beers.

WHAT ACTUALLY IS FORMULA MILK?

Formula milk has actually been around since the 19th century. Before then, if your baby wasn't being breast-fed by its mum, it'd probably have been suckling on the teat of another mother. Formula milk used to be made up of animal milk, and then it was made from evaporated milk, before becoming what we know today as commercial formula milk, which is meant to closer replicate the benefits of breast milk. Formula milk was huge in the 50s and 60s, with reports of more than half of babies being formula fed, before breast feeding made a big resurgence from the 70s.

The infant formula milk given to newborns today is based on cow's milk whey and babies being formula-fed tend to stay on this until they are 6 months old, when solid foods are then introduced. For all this sort stuff, consult the club doctor.

SHOULD I GIVE MY BABY WATER?

Breast-fed babies won't need any additional drinks, although a sip of water through a cup would be fine. The breast milk is all the drink they really need - so no Sheringham–Gazza dentist's chair celebrations required. However, if your little one is on the formula, then they might fancy a bottle of (cool boiled) water, particularly in hot weather to reduce the risk of dehydration – in which case let the celebrations commence!

SOLID FOODS AND WEANING

"When Italians tell me its pasta on the plate, I check under the sauce to make sure"

Alex Ferguson

Footballers are on a much stricter diet than they used to be. Back in the old days there were so many stories of bad diets, excess drinking and debauchery. Things have changed a lot since the 'good old days' and most definitely for the better. Your little footballer has 3 things going for him: there are more healthy options than ever before, there is more awareness of good dieting because of education and he has got you – a truly special coach at Dad FC to steer him down the right path.

WHEN IS MY BABY READY FOR SOLIDS?

Parents tend to start introducing solids to their babies at around 6 months. Your baby will be able to hold their head up right and sit in the high chair unaided. They'll start to gaze over jealously at what you're eating and maybe reach out to grab some something off your plate. When given some food, they're able to move it around their mouth and eat it rather than just push it back out.

You'll get an idea that your baby is ready for trying solids when they are able to pick up food and put it in their mouths independently, and they're able to swallow too. According to The Association of UK Dieticians, the Department of Health recommends breast feeding until 6 months and then the introduction of weaning onto some solid foods as a child's body stores of some nutrients such as iron naturally starts to run out.

HOW WILL MY BABY REACT TO SOLID FOODS?

It's always funny watching your baby's expressions as they take their first slurps of mush. It's normal if they're not interested and don't know why you're sticking a colourful piece of plastic in front of their face, and squashing mess all around their mouth. Expect a lot of mess in the first few months – this period of mess at the dinner table goes on for years to come, so get comfortable having everything covered in mushy carrot.

WHAT SOLID FOOD SHOULD I TRY?

Dad FC is proud of making this part of the day as fun as possible. Not only is dinner time a great chance to bond with your little one, but they can learn from making a hell of a mess and smelling, seeing, touching and tasting these new foods. Yes, there'll be a few Pizza-Gate episodes, where you'll get caked in organic salt-free gluten-free pizza toppings as you walk down the tunnel after a big defeat, and more food will end up on the floor than in your baby's mouth, but this is part of the fun. Getting frustrated and – dare I say – giving the hair-dryer treatment and berating your baby won't encourage them to have a healthy relationship with food and sets a poor example. So sit back and relax, as the messy eating gets started.

HOW MUCH SOLID FOOD SHOULD I GIVE MY BABY?

When you start giving your baby solid food, it's best to start with just a few spoons full of cereal or rice based food mixed in with milk. Then it'll just be the one solid-based meal a day. As little ones don't need 3 square meals, it's more about getting them familiar with eating, as they begin this weaning process. Your baby will still be getting their lion's share of daily goodness from breast-feeding or formula and could be continuing to breast-feeding up to and past their first birthday (that's your call, or more likely, your partner's call).

STARTING LINE-UP – 1ST TEAM OF SOLIDS

Keep this team fresh and mashed up!

Pundit (in a very broad Scottish accent)

"This looks like a very balanced team. From the back, they're in safe hands here. Banana is an ever-present keeper and very handy. He's been excellent in away games too this season. Potato has been playing for the club for donkey's years – he might not be a high-profile player, but he's always teamed up well with carrot. His younger brother sweet potato is new to the team and gives them something different on the right side of defence. There's a solid 3 in the middle of the park with Avocado, Rice and Cereal teaming up. Rice and Cereal don't tend to play together too often and you don't always know what you're going to get with Avocado, so he's probably the weak link in the side today. The attacking duo of Apple and Pear are in excellent form at the moment. Apple just pips Pear as my personal favourite – Apple's a little sharper, but Pear is versatile so they work well together upfront. You know you'll get goals. On the bench, they do have Peach and Melon. These guys would get in most teams but are just being kept out of the starting line up by the in-form Apple and Pear. Broccoli gives them something different in the middle, but he's young and it might be too early to bring him in at this stage. Chicken and Fish could be introduced to the first team soon too. A high quality Jar of Baby Food has been loaned in as a decent alternative."

TRICKS AND TIPS
Keep this team fresh and mashed up!

MANAGER'S TACTICS

- Make the food puree pretty thick and consistent. You can have a few lumps in it, but you want it all to be pretty soft.

- Vegetable puree – mash up carrots, courgettes, peas, potatoes, sweet potato or broccoli.

- Fruit puree – mashed up pears, apples and bananas work particularly well together.

- Cereal into milk – try mashing up a healthy cereal or soft rice into milk.

- Could try introducing things like chicken, mashed up fish, lentils and full-fat dairy products such as yoghurt.

- Try just adding one new thing at a time. Learn the flavours of the food, helps me find out what works and doesn't work, and I can better identify if there's a food allergy!

- Introduce new foods, textures and flavours gradually through the first year (from 6 to 12 months old)

AVOID HONEY, SUGAR, SALT AND NUTS

Babies don't really need additional sugar and salt into their diets – their milk intake covers what they require for this. Nuts can of course be a choking hazard, so if you introduce some nuts from 6 months old, then ensure that you ground down the nuts first. Honey can contain some bacteria which can be particularly harmful for babies under a year old, so best to avoid.

VITAMINS

The Department of Health has recommended that babies from 6 months old have vitamin drops. A healthy supply of vitamins A and C can usually be acquired through a good diet, but it can be difficult to get a decent amount of Vitamin D from food alone. For this reason, the department of health recommends a vitamin supplement which comes in the form of drops and contains A, C & D. Consult your club doctor or health visitor for advice.

KIT NEEDED

- ☑ Small plastic pots or containers (to store purees)
- ☑ High chair
- ☑ Muslin cloths. kitchen roll and wipes
- ☑ Loads of bibs
- ☑ Plastic bowls
- ☑ Plastic plates
- ☑ Plastic cutlery (spoons, soft and round-edged knives and forks)
- ☑ Cup, beaker (or sippy cup)
- ☑ Bottles (you should already have these if you're giving expressed breast milk or formula milk)
- ☑ Washing up sponge and brush (use only for baby's kit)

FOOD SAFETY AND HYGIENE

- Wash your hands and wash your baby's hands before and after eating

- Wash your hands before and after you prep food.

- Wash your hands immediately after touching any raw meat, poultry or eggs and clean surfaces thoroughly too to avoid contamination.

- Wash all bowls and food utensils in hot soapy water after using.

- Ensure food is cooked thoroughly and then cooled before feeding to your baby.

- Test the food yourself before giving to your baby

- Help your baby with food and monitor them. You can teach them to be independent but should always remain vigilant whilst they are eating.

- If pre-preparing meals, cool the food quickly and store it in an airtight container in the fridge. Eat within 2 days. Again, test food yourself before giving your child.

- If you freeze food, defrost thoroughly before use. Defrost only once. Reheat only once. Reheat to the point it is steaming hot throughout, cool it throughout and stir to ensure there are no hotspots, test it yourself, then feed to your little one.

TRICKS FOR FEEDING A BABY

Generally speaking, if your baby is hungry, they will eat. Having said this, there are fussy-eaters and no matter how much of a good eater your baby becomes, there will most definitely be a time when they decide that they just don't want to eat anything. Here are some tried and tested tactics used by other Dad FC coaches.

Distract and blind-side: the classic technique of averting your baby's attention to something other than food. Perhaps you start to pretend the fingers on your empty hand are little birdies jumping up and down. Once you've got the baby's attention, try to get a spoonful in.

Philtrum brush: babies are born with an instinctual reaction to their philtrum being touched. The philtrum is the groove between the base of your nose and the top of the upper lip. Brush the bottom of the spoon on the philtrum and they might inadvertently open their mouth.

Airplane: the 101 of feeding tactics. Pretend the spoon is a jumbo jet coming in to land in your baby's mouth. The longer the flight path the more fun it is. The more fun it is, the higher the chance of a successful landing.

Teddy's hungry too: "What, you didn't know? Oh yea, teddy eats mashed courgette and carrot all the time. Watch…" This might be enough to get your baby to join teddy and tuck into some grub.
Feed daddy: you'll probably be touching on some Freudian issue if you make your baby think that they're actually going to lose their food to you if they don't eat it, but try having a small taste of their food to show them how tasty it really is. The bigger your reaction

to enjoying the food, the better.

Make a sub just before a set piece: they say that a defending team should never make a substitution just before a set piece is taken. Why? Because there's a fair chance that someone won't know who they're meant to be marking, which leads to oceans of space for an attacker to pounce. When it comes to feeding, the opposite is true. Tempt your little one with a spoon full of food they want to eat, then just as they open their mouth, make the substitution and bring on the spoon with the fresh greens that you'd like them to try - a classic decoy.

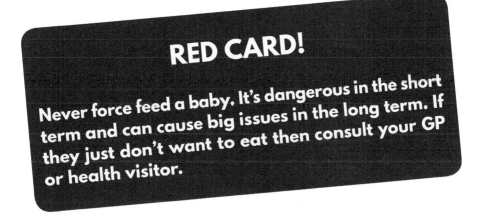

RED CARD!

Never force feed a baby. It's dangerous in the short term and can cause big issues in the long term. If they just don't want to eat then consult your GP or health visitor.

POST–MATCH INTERVIEW

We started our baby off with breast feeding from day one and it was an instant natural bond between mum and baby. It's strange at first seeing your partner just fall into this new role like she knew exactly what to do. There was a little nervousness about whether the baby would latch on (i.e. start sucking) but before you knew it, it was a second nature. Or first nature, I guess. The midwife popped round to check things were going swimmingly and fortunately we were doing OK. Like most parenting things, it didn't go without some hiccups though. After having the baby home for a couple of days, I had a venture out of the house to get some well-deserved fish and chips, only to return to what can only be described as a milky blood bath. Our week old baby had torn open one of her mum's nipples and blood was dribbling everywhere (onto my wife, in the baby's mouth and dripping on the floor). Suffice to say, it looked worse than it was, although having my own mum standing beside me in the doorway, looking at my wife exposing her bleeding breasts was... (whilst you'd think outrageous, and it would be if it happened before having a baby) ... well, I kind of just rolled with it. There was no point in crying over spilt milk.*

*This gag was unsurprisingly lost on my wife and mum at the time. Some people have no sense of humour.

After this, there was the milk-gate scandal. Our baby decided to enter the world during the London 2012 Olympics. This meant we missed watching the amazing feats of Jessica Ennis and Mo Farah, and reluctantly had to give up our tickets to several events, including women's beach volleyball and men's Greco-Roman wrestling. Gutted about giving up the women's beach volleyball tickets; the men's Greco-Roman wrestling... not so much. A few weeks post-birth we decided to venture out to watch some Paralympics events. Leaving the little one at home for the first time was a big deal, but everything was prepared, breast milk had been expressed and we'd only be gone for the afternoon. Oh, we decided to draft grandma in, so that the little one wasn't lonely at home. All was going swimmingly at the Paralympics and my wife was enjoying a well-deserved break. Until nature started to take its course, that is, and breast-milk started to leak, then spray from her bulging breasts. We didn't get to watch the end of the Paralympics table tennis.

6 months later and it was an absolute joy to be giving my baby her first solid foods. The expressions on her little face as she tried new flavours were great, and this represented a real opportunity for me to get more involved in the feeding process than ever before.

06. TRAVEL AND AWAY GAMES

"I could have another moan, but I'm sick to death of my own whingeing"

Steve Bruce

They say that playing away from home is always trickier than playing at home. When it comes to babies, this statement couldn't be truer. Leaving the house can require quadruple the time and effort that it used to before you had a baby. But why does this happen? Why does it take so long to leave the house and can anything be done to reduce this lost time? In this chapter we give you all you need to know about preparing for travelling with a baby.

PLANNING AWAY GAMES

Previously you could grab your keys, wallet and phone and you're off. Once a baby arrives, you need to start thinking about a trip out of the house at least a few hours before, if not days or weeks in advance. Yes, you'll get the occasional blasé pundit (often a hippy grandparent who forgot how stressed they were when they had to look after their own babies) who chucks a bit of advice about just 'going with the flow' and tells you that your baby 'will probably be fine' without a coat and without a changing bag for 'oh just a few hours'. The reality is, a little bit of prep goes a long way. As many Dad FC managers will tell you, failing to prepare, is preparing to fail, so plan and pack bags accordingly.

TRAVEL BAG AND CHANGING BAG ESSENTIALS

Having a changing bag stocked with all the key items is mandatory for all away games. There are extras that you'll need to bring when staying the night too:

☑ Nappies

☑ Baby wipes
☑ Cotton wool
☑ Hand sanitiser
☑ Changing mat
☑ Nappy bags
☑ Cream
☑ Blanket
☑ Muslin
☑ Snacks
☑ Water
☑ Bottle
☑ Milk
☑ Extra set of clothes
☑ Dummy
☑ Sunscreen
☑ Hat
☑ The red book and emergency numbers
☑ Tissues
☑ A toy and/or small book

When packing your bag for nights away, it's common sense to go through your daily routine and pack the everyday items you use. This includes food and feeding / sterilising equipment, clothes and nappies, plus bedtime and bath time essentials. On top of this, some useful extras to think about are: stair gates, first aid kit, plug adapter, travel cot, night light, baby monitor and a car seat.

CAR–SEAT SAFETY

Just as a footballer gets a golden handshake before signing for a new club, your baby needs a car seat before it can come home. There's really only one thing you need to get for the car for a newborn, and that's a car seat. Many retailers of baby car seats now offer fitting services to help you get the damn thing in.

TIP

Always buy car seats from new, rather than second hand otherwise you don't know whether it's already been involved in an accident – it's just not worth the risk. Also check that the car seat has the latest safety regulations (United Nations ECE Regulation number R44.03 or R44.04 or i-size regulation R129 as of March 2016).

PLAN AND PACK WITH THE 5 WS & H MODEL

Who? Who are we going to see? Will there be animals, will there be smokers? Will we be the only people with a baby? Will it be a breast-feeding friendly crowd? Can we leave whenever we need to or would that be rude?

Where? Will there be toilets we can change the little one? Is it baby-proof and baby-friendly? Will it takes ages to get there? Will we be back in time for the sleeping routine?

What? What are we going to be doing when we get there? Will any activity require both our attention, or can one of us look after the baby whilst the other one gets involved in the activity?

When? And for how long? Is it at a convenient time of day so as not to affect routines? When will the baby need feeding, sleeping and changing in the before, during and after periods of the visit? Do we have another event planned that same weekend? Having 2 days out of the house can mean no time for completing the growing list of housework that needs doing!

Why? Do we really want to or need to go? How important is it? Will we actually enjoy it? What other options are there?
How? Are we travelling by car, public transport or walking? Do we have enough petrol, are the trains running, do we need to buy tickets in advance?

And why do we need to think of all of these things? Because you want to avoid the following sorts of situations kicking off...

Situation 1
Your partner crouching in a corner of a friend's kitchen, breast-feeding in front of an awkward room of non-parents, who don't want to look at her but keep looking anyway.

Situation 2
A laissez-faire crowd of friends and friends of friends, who changed 'a quick coffee' into a game of cricket in the middle of the country park because it's scorching weather. You just need to find a place to make formula milk and avoid your baby either being burned by the sun or bludgeoned by a cricket ball. Oh, and you didn't bring the sun cream because it was just going to be 'a quick coffee'.

Situation 3
That family-friend-but-not-really-a-friend has brought along her

friendly Staffie who 'only wants to play' with your baby's face.

Situation 4
A bored, screaming, tired, hungry, thirsty baby who just shat themselves. And you've already used the 2 nappies you brought with you. Oh well, how were you to know you'd actually be stopping by for a couple of hours to visit a step-relative-twice-removed that your parents just have to visit today.

Ultimately, you've got to factor in all of your baby's needs into the Who, What, When, Where, Why and How model and pack the bags accordingly.

WHEN CAN A BABY LEAVE THE HOUSE FOR THE FIRST TIME?

There are no hard and fast rules when it comes to your baby being ready to leave the house. So long as you're taking into account your baby's needs, then it's fine to take them on their first trip to the park or into town from this first week. Some books or resources dictate a lengthy period of time where you shouldn't let your baby leave the house – like a couple of months for example! This would effectively put parent and baby in quarantine and could drive you insane!
Bugs and the change in temperature outside the house are probably the biggest factors to consider, so just check your baby isn't too hot or cold and dress them suitably. It's probably worth putting an extra cardigan and blanket in your bag, just in case you need to add them later. As for the bugs, just try to swerve the pram away from sniffling strangers and cheek-pinchers.

WHAT SORT OF TRIPS SHOULD WE GO ON?

Going for a stroll in the park or a walk to the local shops make for good first trips out. It's wise to make your first few trips small ones. This way you'll get used to packing your kit with the peace of mind that home is just round the corner.

You can then enjoy restaurants, cafes and become acquainted with the local 'mum & baby' groups and soft play areas.

Here are some things to consider when travelling to different places with little ones:

BEFORE YOU ARRIVE

- Is it baby-proof (spacious for buggies, bright rooms and clean tables)?
- Is it welcoming (or does it look too busy, too pretentious for kids or more like the Queen Vic)?
- Is it baby-friendly? Is there a play area? Are there quieter corners in the room for mums who prefer discrete breast-feeding?
- Does the menu have healthy finger food for 6-12 month old babies?
- Is there a back-up plan (if the first restaurant is not up to scratch or unaccommodating)?
- Is it nearby? Can you pop home easily if you need to, or can you prepare for a longer stay?

WHEN YOU ARRIVE

Check out where the toilets are

Don't be afraid to ask for better seats (more comfortable sofa-benches, somewhere you can put the pram, somewhere not so close to the doors or kitchen)

FIND THE HIGH CHAIRS

Pay for the bill at the earliest opportunity after finishing your meal. Forget about social norms – if your baby kicks off and you need to leave, you won't want to be hanging around trying to grab a waiter's attention, when you could have paid up 5 minutes ago and left as soon as you needed to.

ACCOMMODATION

Hotels can be a pain in the arse when you've got a baby. Booked a lovely hotel room? Great. However, once you've put your baby down to sleep in the cot at the end of your bed, where do you go? Equally, you can have the same problem with B&Bs unless your room is right next to a lounge or reception area where you can see your room and no other rooms are closer to yours. Call us paranoid, but it's not worth taking the risk. So, your best option is an apartment, guesthouse or a hotel / B&B room with its own room or balcony for you to give your baby some space and quiet to sleep without you talking nearby (if that helps them sleep better).

You've also got to consider warming milk and baby foods. Not all hotels and B&Bs are accommodating for this, whereas guest houses and apartments usually come with suitable kitchens.

PUSHCHAIR OR PRAM?
THE OPTIONS

Me: "Can you fold a pram whilst the baby is inside it?"
Shop assistant: "No. No, you can't."

Similar to baby bed options, there are several options when it comes to carting your baby around town too.

PRAM

Suitable from birth to early toddler. Prams usually have a lie-flat position for newborns with the baby facing you – sometimes this seat unit is reversible and can also be detachable as its own carry cot (suitable for sleeping). Pram is the sturdiest of the transport options and is also the least foldable (but can often still be folded).

PUSHCHAIR

Usually suitable for newborns as well as older babies. Pushchairs are similar to prams, still very sturdy but often more foldable. Pushchairs usually have reclining and both forward and rear facing options. Pushchairs also come in 3-wheeler options for the trendy toddlers. The 4-wheeler is more suitable for all-terrain.

TWO-IN-ONE TRAVEL SYSTEM

Suitable from birth until toddler. Two-in-ones usually encompass both a pram (lying down base) and a pushchair (forward-facing seat for older babies). For this reason two-in-ones are usually more expensive but they tend to last well into the toddler years.

THREE-IN-ONE TRAVEL SYSTEM

Much the same as a two-in-one with the addition of having a car seat as a third option. This becomes useful if you're embarking on a journey that includes walking and car or train.

BUGGY

Usually suitable from around 6 months old. A buggy is a lightweight option and is often just forward-facing. Buggies take up much less space than prams or pushchairs and can be stored away conveniently. They tend to come with hoods and it's wise to get a rain cover for it too. The ride won't be as smooth as a pram but a buggy is very nimble and good for getting around town and for travelling.

STROLLER

A stroller is the same as a buggy. The manufacturers are just adding complexity and presumably think that 'stroller' sounds cooler than buggy.

SOME SCENARIOS TO THINK ABOUT WHEN CHOOSING TRAVEL EQUIPMENT...

TRAVELLING BY TRAIN

A pram will be too big to bring up the aisle of a train, so you'll have to leave it in the corridor. Even if the carry cot is detachable, it's likely to be too big to take down the aisle to your seat. A detachable car seat allows you to park and fold the travel system's wheels, and take the car seat to your table with the baby still in it.

TRAVELLING BY BUS

You're able to get on the bus OK, but can you navigate between the seats and vertical poles, or is the pram too wide? If there's no space for another pram on the bus, can you wait for the next bus, walk or fold it and hold the baby?

IN THE SUPERMARKET

You need to get washing liquid, fabric conditioner and toilet roll, plus you want to buy that 4 pack of beer for tonight's game - but only have room for 3 of these things in the pram

a)   Leave the beer, you probably won't get a chance to watch the football anyway

b)   Leave the conditioner, the baby's clothes don't need to be that soft

c)   Buy all 4 items and try to carry them and push the pram at the same time

d)   Get a pram with a big basket for storage

OTHER THINGS TO THINK ABOUT WHEN CHOOSING A PRAM?

- Foldable: where and how will you store it?

- Smooth ride: bigger wheels often lead to a smoother ride

- Width: can you get in on a bus or in between narrow aisles?

- Handling: can you push it with one hand if you need to? Does it feel sturdy but easy to steer?

- Storage: will you need somewhere to store things when you're out and about?

- Accessories: will you want a rain sheet or a coffee cup holder?

- Safety: it's passed the safety tests, but do the brakes and safety harness feel secure?

STROLLERS ON A PLANE

How does carrying a buggy work? You can usually drop it at the boarding gate, just before you get on the plane. It will then be put into the hold. It usually doesn't count as normal hold luggage, so there's usually no charge for it. When you arrive at your destination, the buggy may be in the usual baggage collection conveyor belt, or it may be in a special area for oversized baggage.

It's worth getting a buggy bag to put your buggy in – it makes it easier to carry, protects it, and you can also put the rain-cover inside the bag – to avoid losing it or it taking up space in your carry-on luggage

POST–MATCH INTERVIEW

Going to a 'mum and baby' session

Upon entering the 'mum and baby' domain that is Baby Group, I found I was the only dad in the room. It was daunting at first – being the odd one out, with neither me nor the mums knowing quite what the etiquette was. When the event organiser addressed the group as "mums and dad" I felt a strict obligation to show how much fun I was having. I plastered a grin onto my face, which in hindsight probably made me look creepier.

Eventually my face tired, but I felt the need to cement this creepy grin, eventually using a forced yawn to drop the smile.

The sorts of things I got involved with included singing nursery rhymes, holding the parachute which the crawling babies gather under, dancing with a teddy bear (being careful not to smile at the teddy bear) and dancing with my baby (which was actually very fun).

My advice: definitely go to these play groups and, like anything, you'll get more comfortable with them over time.

07. RELATIONSHIP WITH THE HEAD COACH

"I would say that I'm having less sex now that I'm playing in Serie B. There is more to think about in this division"

Gianluigi Buffon

Over the course of this long, challenging first season, both parents will go through a lot together. It's incredible to build a wonderful family with the person you love. It won't all be a bed of roses (the bed might not see much action at all to be honest), but with a bit of love and hard-work, you'll both finish the season as champions. The relationship between mum and dad is arguably as important as the relationship between parent and child. So in this chapter we're focussing on the obstacles that could rear their ugly heads and how to tackle them.

EARLY MONTHS

The relationship between a couple could change massively once they become parents. No longer will they have each other's full attention.

Some people describe the moment when a woman becomes a mum as a light switch moment. Her brain switches into a new maternal mode and there's no stopping it. New dads are dealing with lots of new feelings and concerns themselves, so to find that their partner has changed into a monster can be disconcerting to say the least.

It's like she completely resents me for causing her so much pain!

There could also be a sort of feeling that a new mum doesn't want anyone to come in between her and her baby, and as a dad is literally the closest thing to them – he's sort of in the way.

A newborn baby takes centre stage in the family home and both parents recognise the importance of their newfound roles of nurturing this newcomer. A new mum wants to provide her baby with the most important things the baby needs (e.g. her milk) and the new mum naturally feels that she is the only one who can give the baby everything they need. As a result, instead of all things feeling equal, the new mum may assume power of the family home. Consequently, dads sometimes feel that they can do no right. The sorts of things new dads have said include:

- I just sort of feel in the way. Like I can't really do anything right
- I was washing the dishes and she got annoyed that I wasn't looking after our baby
- I was looking after our baby and she got annoyed that I wasn't washing the dishes
- She is no longer interested in cuddles
- She is no longer interested in sex
- She hates my guts
- I think she wants me dead
- I'm running around the house like a headless chicken and she thinks I'm incompetent
- I sympathetically say 'I understand' and she shouts "How can you possibly understand!?"

Does any of this sound vaguely familiar? Whether any or all of above is true or not, it doesn't really matter. The point is, at some time over the first 3 months of the season, there will likely be some friction between a new mum and a new dad. It's how they deal with it that matters. The simple answer is communication. The complicated answer is that it takes time to work through these issues. Talking things through between each other and having a support system in place (close friends or family to talk to or help with babysitting) can help relieve the pressure new parents feel. Time is also a good healer when it comes to new parenting. Little ones become more independent as they grow; meaning new parents often gradually find each other again, forming a common bond through raising their little one.

HOW WILL MY PARTNER FEEL IN THE FIRST FEW WEEKS?

Her body has been battered and bruised. She's really gone through the wars on this one and every part of her is exhausted. She'll be tired, have an aching body, having not eaten properly for a few days, not had a proper conversation, had a lot of physical and mental stress to get this baby out of the tunnel and onto the pitch for its debut. So yea, she might be feeling a little peaky.

If your partner is feeling the strains of parenthood, then there might not be much you can say that will them happy, but here are some things you should definitely not say:

HOW CAN A NEW DAD HELP A NEW MUM?

Get up in the night – If the baby needs feeding then bring the baby over to her, help the baby latch on, move the baby from one breast to another, burp the baby, change the nappy if needed, put the baby back to sleep.

Get home on time – Don't stay late. Being punctual and keeping promises shows you're someone she can rely on. When you get home from work, take the baby from her (without snatching) and give her some space to do whatever she needs to do. It's likely that she's neither eaten properly nor gone to the toilet since you left this morning!

Do things without asking her permission – Yes, she's become the boss of the house by default, but that doesn't stop you from having all competence whatsoever. This is a new game for both of you, so getting your hands dirty is an important job. You're a manager of Dad FC, not a babysitter, so step up to the plate, without being asked to step up.

Prepare the set pieces – Ensure that bottles, teats and dummies are clean

Be attentive - She could be a bit of an emotional train wreck in the first few months, so being attentive to her feelings is more important now than ever before. Sure, you've been a great partner since you've been together (no one doubts that), but showing affection, kisses hello and goodbye and compliments can go a long way to creating a pleasant atmosphere.

LATER MONTHS

Things may settle down into some sort of new normality now, but don't just expect things to change massively after the 3 month period. For many new parents, it can take over a year before they feel completely into their new roles as parents. What's important is to be empathetic, take the hits and roll with the punches. Try to remember that she chose you to be the father of her babies for a reason. And while it may not seem that she likes Daddy very much at the moment, that will change at some point.

ARGUMENTS

Every couple has arguments, and just because you've become parents doesn't stop you from having them too. Arguing as a parent can feel a bit more intense and more of a bigger deal at first, like you've let yourselves down and didn't know it was going to be like this when you signed up for the role. You wouldn't turn the clock back, but it's damn hard now that it's got going.

Well, as they say, when the going gets tough, the tough gets going. So pack your bags and leave – she can raise your offspring on her own. But hang on just one minute... You don't get out of it this easily coach – managing Dad FC comes with a lifetime contract and you're about to bail out after your first little bust up?! I don't think so. It's time to man-up and accept that things might be a little tougher than you first thought.

The best thing to do in these arguments is to try to detach yourself from your ego. Part of you may want to 'win' an argument, but in reality arguments never really quite work out with a winner and a loser.

See things from her perspective – and don't just pay lip service to her perspective. Actually try to get involved in what's going on in her head, ask her how it makes her feel when you do or don't do whatever pissed her off, and genuinely try to back up her point. You'll find it helps defuse the situation.

Best not raise your voice – you'll only escalate the argument and probably wake the baby in the process.

Try not to dig up the past just to prove a point - You might have some decent examples of where she's wronged you in the past, but bringing these up in the wrong way (even if she's bringing them up) will only serve to boil up the argument further still. Having said this, with a view to getting a resolution that stands the test of time (so you don't start arguing about the same thing again), it's wise to look at previous scenarios and issues to see if there's an underlying error or misunderstanding being made by either of you.

Show respect to her - This can be a bit of a balancing act. Showing respect to your partner shows that you care about her more than you care about winning an argument. So listening to what she says is important. At the same time, you can't roll over and ignore your own feelings – so be honest, see things from her point of view but confirm what you understand and what currently doesn't sit well with you.

Keep resolution focussed - the reason you're both arguing is because you both care about something. If you find that the argument isn't going anywhere, or that it's getting out of hand, it can help to clarify what you both agree on, where you don't see eye to eye, and what are the options for resolving the conflict.

Take a time out - taking a few minutes break from an argument is a great way to take the steam off things. You may come back with fresh perspective, or may even think that the argument wasn't even really worth having in the first place.

So yea, arguments happen when you're a parent, just as they happened before you were a parent too (perhaps more now than they used to). At times like this, sharing experiences with fellow Dad FC managers can be a big help too. You can find these in the form of friends, family members or workmate work mates with kids (basically anyone who's had at least one baby!).

DATE HER

Ah remember those days before you were parents when you could just meet after work and walk along the river or through the park together? It now seems like a bygone era – you reminisce about being able to have a conversation that lasted more than 2 minutes and consisted of no talk about babies.

It's difficult to find the time to plan a date once you're a dad, let alone go on one. When you were together before having a child, you didn't even need to think about it – it just happened. So actually planning something weeks or even months in advance is a brand new habit to adopt, but a very important one.

Ask a close friend, relative or babysitter if they can look after your baby one night and take her out. She may not even feel the need to, and as you're both tired, maybe neither of you will feel 100% fit for a fancy restaurant, but it's good to get something in the diary, no matter how small. Time together as just the two of you is important for your relationship and important for being the great parents you deserve to be.

When you can't get out, because either there's no babysitter, neither of you fancy going out at all, or circumstances just dictate, then make sure you still get a date night in the diary even if you're spending it at home. Cook a decent meal (or grab a nice takeaway if you have to), set the table, put the music on, take a shower and get dressed, and enjoy the evening as if you were in a restaurant. That means no watching TV and no mobile phones. It doesn't take a lot to do this, and you don't need to be out and about in order to have a meaningful evening with your partner.

SEX

After a couple of months many couples are starting to get back into their sex lives, and most couples are right back at it after 4-5 months. The thing with sex problems is that it's often less about the actual sex, and more about the things that lead up to it. If either or both people in a couple are tired or stressed then they're much less likely to feel 'up for it'. If a couple haven't managed to have an conversation that doesn't include talking about the frequency, viscosity or colour of today's baby shit, then they're less likely to feel connected emotionally or romantically. If a couple doesn't give time for holding hands or cuddling each other during the day (without the baby) then why would they expect their sexual relationship to flourish? The first season of fatherhood is partially about trade-offs, and unfortunately for sex, it is often traded-off. Sex comes back over time, as a result of time spent on affection, not instead of it.

AND BY THE END OF THE FIRST YEAR?

A new mum might be more chilled now the little one is more independent. Dare I say it, she may be thinking about Number Two! For now, the focus will most definitely be on creating the biggest and bestest birthday party a 1 year old has ever had...

08. YOU: MANAGER OF DAD FC

"I stopped trying to be beautiful and thought only of being good"

Ruud van Nistelrooy

Throughout the first year of parenthood, you could experience any number of new feelings as a new dad. You'll now be officially a man – a Man Dad, if you will. Most dads (and certainly mums) saw you as a sort of half-man half-boy until the moment your partner gave birth to a tiny baby, who somehow resembled Wayne Rooney more than yourself. At that very moment, when your little Wayne Rooney lookalike popped out of the tunnel and screamed his first scream, you somehow transformed into a completely different identity. That new identity, is of a man who is tired, does more around the house, takes responsibility for a brand new little life, has had their sex life killed, doesn't really look after their health like they used to and has exacerbated their back injuries. Sounds fun, right? The truth is, being a new parent can mean all of these things and more, much more. This doesn't mean it's a bed of roses. Oh no, there are plenty of nasty surprises in store for new dads.

If this hasn't put you off (or if indeed it's too late to put you off), then read on, new manager. For being a manager at Dad FC means embracing each and every one of these challenges. You will learn to love these battles and share stories with other dads about how tough life is and how much spare time you used to have before being a dad. You'll share photos of babies and precious moments as your little one develops over the weeks, months and years to come. It gets better and better.

BECOMING DADDY

There's no doubt that becoming a dad is one of the biggest changes that will happen in your life. It can affect different men in different ways, which is why we've gathered comment from a couple of different dads in order to get two perspectives on the subject of YOU.

Sam – dad to a 1 week old baby girl

Becoming a dad felt surprising normal. You can try to imagine what it'll be like before it actually happens, and you read how life changing it can be, but it really felt natural when it happened. It's like she (my week old daughter) has always been here.

We're still trying to settle into a new sleep pattern and I'm definitely feeling tired. There's more to do around the house now – I'm washing up and sterilising bottles, preparing meals, cleaning the house, feeding the baby, changing the baby and making sure I'm clean too! Our little one didn't take to breast-feeding so we ended up on formula milk alone. This meant a few car journeys to get more supplies.

My partner has just been through a lot with the pregnancy and labour, so I'm naturally taking on more tasks whilst she's recovering. We've also got a dog, Paddy, so I've still got to take him on walks and make sure he's not feeling left out. I'm meant to be studying too, but I'm yet to find any time for this.

My advice would be to try to relax into it and stay calm. You can have little panics, like "She's not breathing! She's not breathing!" when in actual fact she's fine. Stay calm as babies can pick up on your panic. It's weird how distracting my baby can be without her actually doing anything. She makes a small squirming sound or pulls a facial expression and I'm working out what she's trying to tell me. I just stick to the rule of 3 – feed, change or burp.

John: dad to a 15 week old baby girl

The birth was, in my case, pretty shocking and it didn't go to plan. Everything was fine in the end and the baby was healthy but it just took a lot longer than we expected and we didn't get the natural birth we planned for. But actually being dad is quite normal.

I did get a few panics in the first week or so, like the first time I bathed her I wasn't sure if I was holding her correctly and didn't want her to slip. We do have the basics sorted – if she cries I just think about what she's recently done (i.e. has she been cleaned, fed or slept?) and I work through these 3 things, plus winding, to make sure she's happy.

We're doing a mix of breastfeeding and formula bottle at the moment. We share the jobs – so I'm doing a mix of bottle feeding, cleaning the house and preparing meals. There's not a routine for bedtimes yet; she stays with us until we go to bed anywhere between 9:30pm and 10:00pm. I don't tend to get up in the nights as much as my wife because I'm working during the day.

As the labour took so long, I've had to go back to work after our little one has been home for just one week. After a week back at work, I can tell you that it's easier to be at work than it is to be at home! Being able to grab a coffee and eat a hot breakfast is great, so I appreciate how tough it is for my wife at home. As soon as I get home I take responsibilities of looking after the baby or doing whatever housework is needed. Oh, and having my mum here for the first week helped a lot — I advise you to get parents round to help if you can!

MENTAL WELLBEING

"I've slept with a coat hanger in my mouth to keep the smile on my face these last couple of days"

Mick McCarthy

It's normal for new dads to feel run down, especially after being a parent for a few months. This first 3-6 months can be toughest, and many dads say that things start to get a little easier as their babies get towards the one year old milestone. Whilst there's no doubting that even the fittest new dad will get tired and groggy at some point, changing a few habits here and there can have a real positive impact on your mental and physical state.

Being a new dad, your goal has changed. Previously, perhaps you wanted to be fit just for the good feeling and health benefits. Now, you'll want to keep yourself fit and healthy so you can better look after your little one and have enough energy to do all the jobs required around the house. Before becoming a dad, you used to finish work and could relax. Becoming a dad, means that you're effectively continuing your work into the evening and night. OK, the dad-work is completely different to your day-job and should be much more enjoyable and rewarding, but nevertheless, you could find yourself exhausted when trying to juggle your previous responsibilities with your new ones. Here are some small, common-sense tactics that could help work around some of the first-season challenges.

CHALLENGES VS. HOW TO DEAL WITH THEM

- Improve social life? Meet new dads and organise dates with mates well in advance
- Keep in touch with the world and your old hobbies? Get a tablet or subscribe to a weekly paper like The Week to keep up with things whilst you're on the go
- Time flying by and want to do more with it? Take photos and videos: you'll remember how truly amazing this whole experience is and how much you really did enjoy those times. You might be more tired and feel stuck in a bit of a lull on a day to day basis, but reflecting on all the wonderful things you did with your little one and how much they've changed is a great thing to look back on and share with your partner.

STRESS WITH TANTRUMS

"You've got to take the rough with the smooth. It's like love and hate, war and peace, all that bollocks"

Ian Wright

When they say nothing can prepare you for fatherhood, one of the things that catch many new dads out is how excruciating the shrill crying can be as it pounds through your ears. You might be lucky enough to have a quiet baby, or possibly be immune to the cries, but many dads (and mums) find the sound of their own baby cry immediately draining. It's like someone flushes any and all energy that was in your body. Your heart rate goes up, you get cold sweats. Intolerable.

Well the good news is that all of this is perfectly natural and is nature's way of telling you that your offspring needs love and attention. It's OK to feel stressed out by all this crying. It's OK that it makes you feel angry. It's OK that you feel frustrated that you can't soothe your baby's crying – you just don't always have breasts for it. You might be used to being Mr. Perfect at work, but all of a sudden you feel useless and defeated by a small tiny version of yourself.

What's not OK, of course, is to take the anger out on your baby or partner. There's a difference between being angry with a baby crying and being angry with a crying baby. The former is your body's way of urging you to deal with something urgently. The latter is taking your frustration out on your baby, which is not only wrong – it doesn't even make sense.
Babies can't be naughty. Babies can't do bad things. Babies aren't wrong.

Once your baby grows into a 2-3 year old toddler, you might think about disciplining them if they've done something fundamentally wrong, by teaching them the right way to do something and showing that you are disappointed and sad at the way that they've behaved.

Reacting angrily with them would surely only serve to teach them that Dad has lost control and this is how he sometimes deals with situations? You're also much less likely to be consistent (as you're reacting to them based on your immediate emotional response rather than what you think is right for your child). This inconsistency might also send mixed signals about what's right and wrong.

As your little one gets older, you'll be able to have more conversations with them. For now, their way of explaining what they need is to scream the house down. If you're finding it a big challenge, try relaxation techniques and speaking to your partner, friends or a GP.

GOING TO WORK

Get used to functioning on half a tank of energy (and that's on a good day)

HOW A DAD SEES GOING TO WORK

I'm completely knackered. I leave the house, all scruffy and smelly, I grab a coffee to get me going and I then struggle to stay awake. When in meetings, colleagues talk in depth about 'not-important-anymore' tasks whilst I think about how tired I am and that I'm going home to face an even tougher job.

HOW A MUM SEES YOU GOING TO WORK

He skips out the house in the morning before the baby gets up, slamming the door on the way out to ensure that the baby is definitely woken up. He'll then enjoy a nice hot cup of coffee and get to sit down a train and read the paper. Once at work, he exchanges pleasantries with his friends and enjoys adult conversation. He'll sit at his desk and focus on his work, and is only interrupted by colleagues asking if he fancies a cuppa.

These are two sides of the same coin. You will be operating on a maximum of 50% energy and you will probably get used to it. Regarding work, let people know what you can and can't handle and don't be afraid to say 'no' to jobs that look like they're coming your way. At home, talk about how you're feeling, whilst being authentically empathetic to the mum's situation too.

PHYSICAL WELLBEING

"People in the street tell me to eat less, but I look in the mirror and I look OK."

Ronaldinho

It's obvious that dads have less time for themselves than they used to have pre-fatherhood. All too often, the trade-off is less time spent exercising and more quick meals and junk food. Combine this with a slowing metabolism and developing a Dad-Bod can feel like a fact of life rather than a choice. However, there are small things dads can do to eat healthier, exercise more and keep the pounds from piling up.

TACTICS FOR EATING (AND DRINKING) BETTER

- Avoid fast-food on the way to work. Opt for porridge with banana instead. Buy the multi-packs of porridge sachets if that makes it quicker and more convenient for you (it's still cheaper and healthier than buying food on the go).
- Buy sparkling water instead of sugary fizzy drinks – it still gives you a fizzy kick without all the sugar high and impending come-down.
- Put fruit or nuts on your desk and avoid snacks or the sandwich man
- Cook extra large meals on Sunday and early in the week and use for lunches at work
- Download and use the Drinkaware app – it's easy to use and it'll help you monitor how many calories you're consuming when you drink.
- Buy yourself a big bottle of water and keep it with you at work. Drink regularly and if you ever think you might eat because you're bored, take a gulp of water instead.
- Use a smaller plate when eating your meal at home

TACTICS FOR EXERCISING MORE

- Do push-ups, sit-ups and squats before you take a shower – try to increase the number of reps you're doing
- Do a few stretches when you're in the shower
- Take a brisk walk at lunch time
- Walk instead of catching the bus
- Walk up the escalator instead of standing on the side

- Set goals: can you get a couple of short runs in each week? Mark them down on your calendar
- Sign yourself up for a 5k or 10k and run it for charity to force yourself to be accountable
- Do a standing workout at home – check out the workout videos on YouTube.

These are just some things that have worked for us. As with all of our advice, it's not to be taken as medical or health advice. Always speak to a healthcare or medical professional for any medical, health, physical wellbeing and exercise advice.

CRAZY GANG APPROACH TO PARENTING

In football, some clubs have all the resources and all the money and all the players they could possibly ever wish for. It almost seems harder for these clubs to lose games than it does for them to win them. Take Chelsea and Manchester City for example. The oligarch Roman Abramovic and Sheikh Mansour ploughed so much money into their respective squads that surely any manager could win things at the helm.

Unless you have the luxury of 2 nannies, 2 cleaners, 2 sets of grandparents, a personal GP, personal trainer and a personal shopper to buy all of your babies products with your limitless supply of cash, then you're going to need to play this game a little differently to the Manchester Citys and Chelseas of this world. You're going to need to play this game, just how Wimbledon's Crazy Gang of the 80s and 90s played.

Wimbledon's Crazy Gang were known for their straight-forward and direct playing style. It was this style of play that successfully took them from the bottom tier of the football league, right up to the Premiership, where they were able to mix it with Liverpool and the other big boys. When it comes to being a parent, there are so many new challenges for you to face, and you'll be facing all of these at the same time.

There are new things to manage, like changing, bathing and feeding a baby, as well as continually shifting your tactics for soothing your baby and getting them to sleep. The goal posts get moved, almost daily. What worked yesterday, doesn't work anymore. If you add in your growing list of responsibilities such as more cleaning, more shopping, more washing and your day job, and it can feel as if you've a mountain to climb – and that's effectively what Wimbledon did as they went from Division 4 in 1982-83 to finishing 6th in Division 1 (top flight) in 1986-87.

Perhaps more impressive, is that they went from non-league football to winning the FA Cup in just 11 years. They achieved these incredible feats without ever changing their direct style, and we'll now show you how you can copy this style to win as a manager of Dad FC.

PLAY DIRTY

Screw your former-self. Your family doesn't need you to wear the smart shirt and tie, be permanently clean-shaven and wear polished shoes every day. Something's gotta give!

Vinnie Jones epitomized Wimbledon's Crazy Gang's tough image. He has received the fastest booking in history (a yellow card 3 seconds into an FA Cup tie vs. Sheffield United) and was sent off no less than 12 times in his career. Patrick Vieira and Roy Keane had 15 red cards between them in Premier League history, so that goes a long way to explain Mr Jones' hard man image.

Welshman Vinnie Jones wasn't the only player at Wimbledon who liked to play rough and ready football. John Fashanu, Dennis Wise and several others were all known to get stuck in and weren't afraid of a tackle. It was very much a case of doing what it takes to win a game. Come hell or high water, Wimbledon would lay it all on the line for the cause.

The reality is, Wimbledon focussed only on the things which would lead to victory and cut the crap out. As Bobby Gould described once their strategy in an interview with Talksport, joking "...goal keepers who can kick the ball 90 yards and a 6-foot 2 bloke to head it in". It might not have looked pretty, but it was pretty effective.

As manager of Dad F.C., you have to focus on the stuff that really matters, and de-prioritise or ditch the things that just don't help you achieve the most important stuff.

PRIORITISE THE IMPORTANT STUFF AND CUT THE CRAP

1. The things that are most important include your baby's health, eating healthy food, a clean baby, a well-slept baby and a comfortable baby.

2. A close second to this are your partner's and your needs. Without looking after yourselves well, how can you expect to be able to have the energy and stamina to look after your little one? So your most important needs are probably sleeping, eating and cleanliness. Then things like social life and exercise come in (both of which are important, but not as important as eating and sleeping).

3. Now with lists 1 and 2 – just focus on 'what it takes' to achieve these things to an acceptable levels.

ASK YOURSELF THESE 3 QUESTIONS...

Question 1

You wake up in the morning after a terrible night's sleep (or lack of...) and all your shirts have creases in them and your shoes are a mess. Do you a) iron a shirt and polish your shoes or b) grab yesterday's sweater or a t-shirt, wear a pair of smart jeans and trainers?

Question 2

It's a mega busy week at work and at home. Do you a) go unshaven for 3-5 days or b) continue to shave as normal?
Answer: a) Come on!? There's no way that you can't go a few days without shaving! Besides, some women love the rugged look.

Question 3

You're just about to nip out of the house with the little one, everything's ready to go and you realise you can't find the blanket that you usually wrap over the top of your little one, though it's not really cold out anyway. Do you a) use a muslin square today instead of the blanket that you can't find or b) start looking round the house for the blanket as you know its somewhere, but just don't know where. Answer a) well done again. The correct answer is a. If it's not so cold that the extra warmth for the blanket vs. the muslin is necessary, then just grab the bloody muslin and head for the door.

I know this short Q&A is mind-numbingly simple but that's intentional. It's infuriating how many people out there make very inefficient choices throughout their daily lives. Dads can't afford to make inefficient choices. Managers of Dad F.C. don't have the extra resources to waste.

PLAY THE LONG-BALL AND CUT OUT THE MIDDLE MAN

Wimbledon manager Dave Bassett championed the long-ball game that became synonymous with the Crazy Gang. He knew that Wimbledon couldn't beat the likes of Liverpool, Arsenal and Manchester United by emulating their styles of play; Wimbledon just didn't have the technical quality to play "good football". This meant that building from the back, wing-play and tikka-takka passing was off the drawing board. Do what you need to do to score goals and win games.

For you, as manager of Dad FC, this means making the right sacrifices, at the right time, without losing focus on what's important. You have to be direct and not waste any time, money or space – as each one of these will become ever more limited once you're a parent: Here are some examples of where you can cut out the middle man (i.e. wasted time and energy) to make your parenting more efficient.

GET THINGS DONE IN A LEAN WAY

- Choose quick healthy snacks instead of taking your time on a nice big well-seasoned lunch.

- Buy all of the same cutlery, bowls, plates, bottles, cups, beakers and dummies so that they are stackable and the parts of any 1 beaker or bottle will fit with any other beaker or bottle.

- Choose to put your little one in practical clothes rather than picking out a certain pink frilly dress with bunny rabbits on it that needs matching tights

- Buy 1 multi-purpose travel system rather than a separate baby car seat, old school pram, toddler pushchair and toddler buggy.

- When packing on holiday, sacrifice bringing 7-10 reading books for baby's bedtime when just 2-4 will do. And opt for small paperbacks rather than large hardbacks. The same goes for toys. You are just wasting space otherwise.
    - Buy yourself a tablet - This is a controversial one, but you still need to communicate with the outside world, look things up online and buy stuff. Turning on a laptop and sitting in the corner of the room just isn't practical when you have a baby to look after.

- If you need your electronics with you, bring a kindle or small tablet rather than a laptop.

- Buy e-books rather than paperbacks (never buy hardbacks

– you will never travel with a hardback book again).

- As you walk through the house from one set piece to another, grab any item in your path that's not in its rightful place and take it with you; drop it off, as close to where it belongs, on the way. Note that the items you pick up need to be in your path and you shouldn't go right out of your way to put them away – you need to maintain a flow.

- When your baby is in the bath, if she has long hair, then wash, condition, dry and plait her hair whilst she's in the bath. That's much faster than doing it outside the bath when she can run-around. Oh, and brush her teeth when she's in the bath too.

The big and the small changes all add up, and the biggest reward you get for this is TIME.

This doesn't mean that there has to be a compromise on end-result. You can still (100%!) look after your baby properly and account for all of their needs, it just means that you're working in a more efficient way – and you can spend time with the people you love and on the things you need to do, rather than running around like a headless chicken.

MASTER THE SET PIECES

During the era in which Wimbledon won the FA Cup, they had truly mastered their set pieces. Dennis Wise was one of the best crossers in the English game, and both Sanchez and Fashanu had great strength and presence to get on the end of corners and free kicks. The result of practicing these set pieces for long and hard hours paid off in spades, when Sanchez met a Wise free kick at Wembley to score what turned out to be the winner against Liverpool in the FA Cup final.

If you can master the following important set pieces then you'll go a long way to having a successful first season at Dad F.C.

1. Feeding
2. Changing
3. Winding
4. Bath
5. Sleep

BE 'LUCKY'

Pundits and players alike would say that Wimbledon were lucky to go all the way in the FA Cup and beat Liverpool 1-0 in the final. The truth is, they worked very very hard and found ways to beat teams which were better than them on paper – and that's smart. The players worked hard on the training ground and Dave Bassett and Bobby Gould were astute coaches with tactical nous that came from testing and learning. As the two sayings go: "*You make your own luck*" and "*The harder I work, the luckier I seem to be*". Work hard at being a dad and you'll have energy and time required to do all the things a parent needs to do.

FROM THE TERRACES

"Can dads get post-natal depression?"

You're probably used to hearing about post-natal depression (commonly shortened to PND) in new mums, however new dads are also susceptible to PND. It would appear that PND in dads can be brought on by a strained relationship with their partner and there's also a link between a dad experiencing depression and his partner experiencing depression. Anxiety about the new responsibility and the financial pressures parenting can bring, are also causes of PND in dads. The symptoms of PND in dads are much the same as they are in mums, and include feelings of guilt, anxiety, inadequacy, despondency, exhaustion, harm, always wanting to cry, comfort eating, obsessive fears, panic attacks, difficulty sleeping and several other related symptoms. If you think you have post-natal depression, or feel that you need support with your mental wellbeing, then try to speak to a close friend, relative or a GP. Taking small steps to adjust your daily life, like exercising and making time for yourself, could help improve mental wellbeing too. If you see a GP about PND they should be able to advise on what steps to take. Treatment for PND could include counselling, therapy, cognitive behavioural therapy, attending support groups and / or medication.

09. INJURY TIME

"Ian Pearce has limped off with what looks like a shoulder injury"

Tony Cottee

Fortunately, most babies' injuries are more Cristiano-Ronaldo-style than Dave-Buust-style and by that we mean tripping over their own shoelaces rather than suffering complete leg breaks. That being said, even when your baby is tiny, there are still plenty of ways they can worry you with injuries and ailments, and what with them not being able to communicate exactly what's wrong with them, it can be daunting. Often it's first a matter of checking symptoms (like your baby's temperature) and then taking steps according to what you find. Here are the Dad F.C. top tips that I do to cope with injury time.

I want to share some basic things which have worked for me, as a parent, or things that I have been informed about but thankfully not had to deal with myself. None of this book (including this chapter) in any way constitutes medical advice or any other professional advice. If advice or expert assistance is required then the services of a competent professional should be sought. If you're ever in doubt about the health of your child, seek medical advice from a doctor. We also recommend buying a decent first aid book and taking a baby first aid course which can be done through NCT, Red Cross or St. John's Ambulance.

HE'S TAKEN A KNOCK! BRING ON THE PHYSIO!

Millions of babies and little children suffer bangs, bumps and bruises every year. There isn't much I can do to prevent my little one falling over (other than some #EpicDadSaves) – and these occasional bumps and bruises happened frequently as my little one started to crawl around the house and increasingly once she began walking at the end of her first year.

Prevention is better than cure, but once the basic baby-proofing is done, if a little one wants to run full force into a door, then it's tough to stop it from happening. The more a baby starts moving around, the more you will see danger everywhere. For the common bumps and bruises, get a First Aid kit. You can get one of the regular green ones, or many pharmacies have special Baby First Aid kits too. Here are basic things you'll want in your kit:

THE DAD F.C. DOCTOR'S KIT BAG (YOUR FIRST AID KIT)

- Tweezers in case your little one gets a splinter
- Gel pack (to keep in the fridge) and apply to bumps
- Pair of scissors for cutting dressings and plasters
- Painkillers / medicine: get an age-appropriate painkiller such as paracetamol or ibuprofen.
- Dosing-syringe and spoon as 2 options for giving medicine to your baby
- Antihistamine cream for insect bites to reduce swelling
- Antiseptic wipes to clean any open wounds and prevent infection
- Antiseptic cream or spray to apply to cuts or burns to prevent infections
- Saline solution and an eye bath: in case they get grit in their eyes
- Plasters in a variety of sizes
- Sterilised gauze dressings for larger cuts
- Bandages for slings or supporting strain injuries
- Sticky adhesive tapes for holding dressings in place
- Thermometer (a digital in-ear or under-arm thermometer)

> **TIP**
>
> Keep your kit in the same place in your home, out of the reach of children and top-up your supplies. Check use-by dates too.

WHAT DO I PLAN TO DO, IF MY BABY...

...HAS GOT A HIGH TEMPERATURE

A normal temperature in babies is about 36.4C but it can vary from one baby to another. What one might call a high temperature depends on the age of a child, but the NHS states that a temperature above 37.5C in a child under 5 years old is a fever. I'd usually be able to feel that my baby is quite warm or hot to the touch, especially on her forehand, and she may appear lethargic, sweaty and red-cheeked.

- Check my baby's temperature using a thermometer, preferably a digital thermometer which is relatively cheap and available from pharmacies. If she is unenthusiastic about me putting the thermometer in their ear, then I try taking my own temperature to reassure them – remembering to replace the lens filter (small plastic cap) after I've used it to avoid transferring germs around the family. Alternatively I use the under-arm thermometer. Both thermometers are effective and I find it useful to take a temperature more than once and go with the highest reading (not the average)

- If my baby has a temperature above 37.5C then encourage her to drink plenty of water or milk

- I regularly check on her and try to keep her at a comfortable temperature (trying to avoid layering her up and trying to avoid removing all layers)

- I might give my baby paracetamol at the dose specified on the bottle or packaging.

- I'd get medical advice from a GP or the NHS if
    - She is under 3 months old and has a temperature of 38C or higher
    - She is 3-6 months old and has a temperature of 39C or higher
    - She is older than 6 months and has a temperature of 40C or higher

...IS HAVING A FIT, CONVULSION, HAS TURNED BLUE, RIGID OR FLOPPY

- I'd lay my baby down on a) on her side to prevent choking b) if choking then I'd follow the choking procedure.
- I'd make sure my baby is cool – not too warm nor too cold

- Fits often last up to 3 minutes. I'd reassure my baby during this time and keep calm myself

- If the fit is still ongoing after 5 minutes then I'd call 999.

- If the fit has stopped (and it's my baby's first fit) then I'd take them to A&E. I'd always tell my GP about any fits my child has.

...IS CHOKING

- If I was not able to see the object in her mouth, then I'd not put my finger or an object into her mouth to try to dislodge it, as I may push the object further down.

- If my baby can't cough, cry or breathe then I'd try to dislodge the object using back blows and chest thrusts. If my baby is coughing loudly then I'd encourage her to carry on coughing.

- I'd check my baby's mouth to see if it's blue, as this is a sign of choking. If her mouth isn't blue, this doesn't mean that she isn't choking.

- **Administer back blows**: Turn my baby upside down, along my thighs and (supporting her head with my hand) I would deliver 5 back blows to the centre of her back with my hand. These are called back blows.

- If the object hasn't dislodged, then I'd check her mouth and if I can see the object, I'd try to remove it using my finger and thumb.

- **Administer chest thrusts**: If the object still isn't dislodged then I'd lay my baby face-up along my thighs, take 2 fingers and place in the middle of her chest (on the breastbone in between the nipples) and push in and up in a thrusting motion 5 times. I'd plan to compress the chest by about a third. These are called chest thrusts.

- I'd check my baby's mouth for the object and remove it with my finger and thumb if I can see it.

- If the object still isn't dislodged after 3 cycles of back blows and chest thrusts then I'd call for an ambulance and continue to do the back blows and chest thrusts until the ambulance arrives.

...HAS HAD A BUMP OR BRUISE

- I'd try to remain calm and reassure my little one. If it's her first bump, it can be disconcerting but I should expect more to come as she begins to tear around the house.

- I'd apply a cold, damp flannel or chilled gel pack to the bump.

- Trust my instinct. More often than not, a small bump is nothing to worry about and there's no serious damage (I must have fallen on my head hundreds of times as a child and I've turned out... actually, scrap that...), but I'd monitor my baby over the next 24 hours for headache, dizziness, vomiting or bleeding and I'd go to A&E or call 999 if there are any serious and significant symptoms.

...HAS SUFFERED A CUT

- I'd gently wash the cut area with an antiseptic wipe.

- If there's loads of bleeding then I'd press on the wound using a clean cloth until the bleeding stops.

- If the cut is on a limb then I'd lift the limb to further reduce bleeding (so long as I'm sure the limb isn't broken).

- After cleaning with the antiseptic wipe, I'd let the wound dry then cover it with a dressing. If it's a small cut then a plaster will do.

- If the wound doesn't stop bleeding and/or there is something in the wound, then I'd go to A&E or ring NHS.

...HAS SWALLOWED TABLETS OR MEDICINES SHE SHOULDN'T HAVE BEEN TAKING

- I'd first look for the missing (supposedly swallowed medicine) to check whether it has been swallowed.

- If swallowed, I'd take my baby to the nearest GP or A&E with the tablets or medicine label with me.

- I'd try to keep myself and my child calm.

...HAS SWALLOWED A POISONOUS CHEMICAL OR A SMALL BATTERY (LIKE THE SMALL, ROUND SILVER ONES)

- Get my child to A&E immediately.

- If possible, I would plan to bring or write down the name of the chemical she's swallowed.

...HAS GOT SOMETHING STUCK UP HER NOSE OR IN HER EARS

- I'd take her to A&E or the minor injuries unit. Trying to remove the object myself could further lodge the object in the nose or ear.

...HAS SUFFERED A BURN

- I'd put the burn under running cold water to reduce the heat (not for longer than 10 minutes).

- I'd cover the burn with a clean cotton (non-fluffy) tea towel or pillowcase. If there are clothes stuck to the skin then I won't try to remove them.

- If the burn is severe, then I'd see my GP or go to a minor injuries unit or A&E.

...HAS BROKEN A BONE

- If I thought that my baby's head or neck is injured then I'd call an ambulance and wouldn't move her as this movement could cause paralysis.

- Signs of a broken arm or leg include large swelling, lots of pain and the limb sticking out at a strange angle.

- Unless I can easily move my baby without causing her pain, then I'd call an ambulance.

- If I can easily move my baby without causing her pain then I'd use my hands to support above and below the injury (to stop movement) and take her to hospital.

- If my baby is in pain then I might give them paracetamol or ibuprofen. I'd avoid giving ibuprofen if my baby has breathing difficulties.

COLDS, FLU, SICKNESS & COLIC

Most babies will pick up some bugs at some point, and as soon as the little one goes to nursery, a runny nose can seem like a family trait, with mum, dad and child all snivelling their way through the year. The good news is that babies often have extremely good bouncebackability, to use a phrase coined by Iain Dowie. A common cold might knock them down first thing in the morning, but by 10am they're as right as rain. Babies will also build up their immune system to fight off more colds as they get older.

COLDS

- Common colds tend to last for about a week.

- I regularly wash my hands to stop viruses from spreading.
- I try to give my baby more fluids if she has a cold.

- I might give her paracetamol or ibuprofen (but I'd avoid ibuprofen if she had breathing difficulties).

- A cold is caused by a virus (not bacteria) so there is no need for me to get antibiotics (which fight off bacteria, not viruses).

- I might try using nasal saline drops, which makes my baby's nose runnier and can also make her sneeze. This can help unblock her nose to help her breathe or sleep better.

COUGH

- Most coughs are just mucus running down the back of a baby's throat during a cold, so as long as my baby is feeding and breathing normally, then a cough on its own is not something I'd worry about.

- I'd make sure my little one gets plenty of rest.

- I'd see a doctor or call a GP if:
    - My baby has a bad cough that isn't going away
    - My baby is also wheezy, breathless and has a high temperature (she could have a chest infection)

- Cough mixtures specifically for babies over 3 months old are available from pharmacists.

CROUP

- Croup is often described as a barking cough, but other symptoms also include a sore throat, runny nose, high temperature and a hoarse voice.

- Keep my baby hydrated.

- Give her plenty of rest.

- I could use paracetamol to reduce her temperature.

- If the condition worsens or doesn't go away after a couple of weeks then I'd seek medical attention. I'd seek medical attention immediately if my baby has severe difficulties with breathing, can't feed or has a very high temperature.

EAR INFECTION

- Symptoms for an ear infection include fever, crying and difficulty feeding. Ear infections often come off the back of a cold.

- It can be difficult to know if a baby has an ear infection, although an indicator is if they're rubbing their ears.

- Most ear infections will clear up on their own after a few days.

- Ear infections shouldn't be treated with drops, cotton buds or anything else in the ear, unless advised by a doctor. When I was a small child, a doctor once told me "don't put anything smaller than your elbow in your ear". I had tried to clean my ear out with a tiny piece of soap after being told by my dad to 'clean your ears out!' having not heard him. Not a good idea. Just saying...

COLIC – WHO THE HELL COINED THE PHRASE "SLEEPING LIKE A BABY"?!

Colic is basically a word for intense crying that often lasts for a long time, with the baby seeming inconsolable. This can be a hugely challenging time for parents and is exacerbated because colic tends to occur during the nights as well. If my baby has colic then I wouldn't think it is something to worry about and I'd think it will pass (even though I've heard it can go on for several hours – yes, hours).

- Colic tends to occur in babies from 0-6 months old and normally stops from around the 4-6 month period.

- Symptoms include prolonged crying even if I've done my set pieces (feeding, changing, winding etc.)

- Whilst there isn't one simple solution to colic (and there is no cure), the main thing is to try to comfort and be there for my baby.

- Swaddling and rocking her in a calming environment (gently lit and with relaxing sounds) could help them to soothe her.

- I could try giving her a warm bath, with gentle back rubs.

- I could try changing her feeding habits a little, such as using a different sized hole in the bottle teat, holding her upright during a feed or extra-long winding after feeds.

- I'd ask for support from (and be supportive to) my partner. I know that sounds like a 'teaching to suck eggs' thing; but it's more of a note to myself that colic can be a distressing time, so it helps if we both feel part of a team. My partner's and my wellbeing is important and rest is priority number 1, so we should be get some shut-eye as and when we can – even if it's at the expense of missing a big game on TV or cleaning the kitchen.

- Colic eventually goes away on its own over time, but if I was finding it a big challenge to cope (and that's absolutely fine) and if I have concerns with it, then I'd speak to a GP or pharmacist for advice.

- Cry-sis.org.uk is a charity who offers support to families with excessively crying babies. It's also has a helpline of trained volunteers to help give advice and reassurance when dealing with crying and sleepless babies.

These are just a few of the ailments that babies can get. Unfortunately there are more nasties out there, including diarrhoea, flu, constipation, dehydration, nappy rash, vomiting, pneumonia, meningitis, measles or chicken pox to name just a few. Invaluable resources of information for all of this are the NHS and medical or healthcare professionals.

FROM THE TERRACES

"How do you know if your baby has colic, reflux or gas?"

Test and Learn is a good approach to colic. If my baby has gas, then winding her will help stop the crying. If she has reflux, then I'll probably see her bring up some milk when I wind her.

"When do you get immediate medical help?"

I don't have an exhaustive list, but some symptoms that I would immediately get medical help from A&E or a doctor include a fit, bleeding in poo, not waking up, very floppy and weak, having a fit, breathing problems, very pale or blue skin, a temperature above 38C if my baby is under 3 months old, above 39C if she is 3 to 6 months old and above 40C if she is over 6 months old.

BABY-PROOFING

Once my baby started moving, I realised how injury prone she was. Think Theo Walcott, Michael Owen, Wes Brown, Andy Carroll, Kieron Dyer, Ledley King, Owen Hargreaves, Jonathan Woodgate, Jack Wilshere, Dean Ashton and Darren Anderton all rolled into one. That's more than enough for an England team there! They're just missing a goalkeeper, which brings us nicely on to you, Mr. Safe Hands.

So let's start with the different parts of the stadium which need to be Michael-Owen proofed before your little one starts diving all over the place:

THE MANAGER'S OFFICE

- Start licking the hair dryer
- Stick his fingers in the plug socket
- Smash his head on the side of the table
- Tip hot coffee over himself
- Smash his head into the trophy cabinet

THE PENALTY BOX

This area is where players are most prone to flailing about like a fish out of water.

- Catch his fingers or get a splinter from a gap in the woodwork – sand and fill

- Get tied up in the loose netting. Remove, tighten or swap with close-knit net
- Lay in the puddle

KITCHEN & CAFETERIA

- Put the pump adapter in his mouth
- Get tangled up in the headphone wire
- Get tangled up in the snood
- Tip the boiling hot water on top of himself
- Tip the bin over on top of himself and start to eat the rubbish
- Knock a plate onto the floor and cut himself on the broken shards

SHOWERS

- Try to drink the hair growth lotion
- Put the head band round his neck
- Swallow a nasal strip
- Get tape stuck on him
- Stick his fingers in the vapour rub and lick them
- Play in the dirt, take off a loose stud and try to eat it

READY TO START BABY PROOFING?

Select one of the injury-prone players mentioned (pick a player, any player), let's take Michael Owen for example, dive onto the floor, start rolling around and see what might inadvertently cause you injury. An innocent gap in the floorboards? A nasty looking nail in the skirting board? A pen lid under the TV cabinet?

You'll need to buy plug socket covers, soft corner edge protectors and a fireguard if you have a fireplace.

Whatever you do to protect your baby, they will find a way to put themselves in peril, just like the aforementioned players. Whilst all of these players can, and have been substituted off many times, there is no substitute for your little star striker, and there is absolutely no substitute for keeping a watchful eye on him at all times.

10. THE LOAN SYSTEM (CHILDCARE)

"Some people believe football is a matter of life and death. I am very disappointed with that attitude. I can assure you it is much, much more important than that"

Bill Shankly

Giving your little one to someone else for them to look after, even for just a few hours, can be a daunting process. Your baby is the most important thing in your life, so it's natural to feel a bit nervous.

However, just as there comes a point in every career when a player considers a move to another club (perhaps they're getting itchy feet, wondering if the grass is greener on the other side, or are getting excited about joining the big leagues of pre-school), your little one has cut their teeth at home and there'll most definitely come a time when you're going to loan them out to a childminder.

BALANCING WORK, CHILDCARE AND MONEY

Where to start?! Going back to work and balancing childcare can be an absolute minefield. I hope I can simplify this sometimes complicated time by suggesting a few things to take into consideration. We're going to look at a few variables and how they interplay with one another. For the sake of simplicity, I'm using the example of a family where the one parent is already back at work (let's called them a nice unisex name like *Ashley*), and the other is just about to go back to work full-time (to avoid conflict, they're called *Pat*). Let's make a sweeping generalisation that *Ashley* is already back at work and *Pat* is considering whether to go back...

SURVIVE ON JUST ONE SALARY ALONE?

If they're trying to work out if *Pat* should go back to work, then the first thing the family has got to work out is if they can afford to live on *Ashley's* salary alone. If they can't, well then there's a high chance that Pat is going to have to go back to work (whether he or she likes it or not).

Let's take the following 2 common scenarios.

Common scenario 1) *Pat* needs to go back to work because the family can't afford to live on *Ashley's* salary alone. At this point, unless the family can get free childcare (e.g. from a grandparent), is against childcare altogether for personal reasons and/or the family is pro *Pat* staying at home, then *Pat* goes back to work full-time. There's also the middle ground... can the family afford *Pat* to go back to work part-time if they'd prefer *Pat* spent more time with the baby?

Common scenario 2) The family can afford to live on *Ashley's* salary alone, but they will make a decent amount more money if *Pat* goes back to work, so they've decided that it's worth *Pat* considering going back to work. In order to come to the conclusion that it's financially worth *Pat* going back to work, the family have to make a simple calculation:

Pat's salary (let's say £1600 take-home pay) minus *Pat's* travel costs, extra work costs (i.e. coffees and lunches) and the required childcare costs (let's say a total of £1100 in costs). Once they have this sum of money (£1,600 - £1,100 = £500), then they can answer the question: is it worth going back to work?

They might also bear 2 other things in mind at this stage. 1) are they happy for their baby to go to childcare (i.e. to develop social skills, play with other kids etc.) and 2) would the family prefer Pat to stay at home if he or she could? This is sort of the same question, just 2 ways of looking at it.

This is a similar to scenario 1 here, but with the difference being that in this scenario (scenario 2), the family can afford for *Pat* not to go to work if they're really against putting their baby into childcare. To make the decision, they just need to value childcare v the extra money coming in. The decision is simple:

EITHER:
Make £500 amount more per month, but *Pat* spends 5 less days a week with the baby, plus the baby is in childcare.

OR

Earn £500 less per month, but *Pat* spends 5 more days with the baby and the baby isn't in childcare.
Again, the middle ground is to look working part-time and reflecting this in the above calculation on take-home salary and costs.

The above either makes perfect sense and clears everything up for you, or it's just a long-winded way of saying...

Extra money in v *Pat* staying at home

QUESTIONS TO ASK YOURSELF BEFORE INTERVIEWING CHILDMINDERS

If you're looking for a childminder, then a little bit of prep goes a long way. Think about what is most important for you as a family, what you can compromise on, and what sort of person you'd like to look after you baby.

Is it important whether we already know the childminder or not?

No, it's fine whether you choose a childminder that you already know (a family friend for example) or find someone completely new. Some parents prefer to use a childminder they already you know – this way they feel a little safer leaving their prized possession with them for the first time. However, it's good to note that childminding is still a business, so by choosing a friend, you're mixing business with pleasure. Perhaps try asking local friends if they know of any childminders in the area.

What are the logistics to and from the childminder's house?

You might find the perfect childminder, but if they live miles away from your house, then is it really feasible to travel there? Think about your commute to and from the childminders – will you be happy to do that commute regularly? If so, ask the childminder if your preferred pick up and drop off times are OK with them. Also check the costs if you're asking the childminder to work outside their regular hours.

What sort of style are we looking for?

When we say style, we're not talking about the childminder's dress sense. It's definitely worth having a chat with your partner about what exactly you're looking for in a childminder. It's easy to make an assumption about what you want in a childminder, only to find out later that you and your partner are looking for a different kind of person to look after your child. By which time, you might have agreed terms with the childminder and have to start the whole process over again. Stressful! So, are you happy with someone who is a little carefree or would you prefer them to be over-vigilant. Are you looking for a loving, grand-motherly figure or a dedicated professional who is Montessori-trained? By the way, the two are not mutually exclusive and there is no right or wrong answer to this (you've just got to find a childminder that feels right for you and your child).

Clarity of expectation

This is a hugely important point, but one that is often overlooked. By 'clarity of expectation' we basically mean that you and the childminder are honest with each other and tell each other anything that you think might affect the childcare arrangement. By asking the questions in this chapter and reading the childminder's contract carefully, you can both be clear on what to expect from each other.

USEFUL QUESTIONS TO ASK WHEN INTERVIEWING CHILDMINDERS

- **Talk me through a normal day.**

- **Where will my little one sleep?**

- **What toys do you have?** You're looking for age-appropriate toys when you ask this one. It's also good to know that there is a decent range of play equipment, to help your little one work on both their fine motor skills (picking up small things) and gross motor skills (using arms and legs).

- **Do you attend playgroups?** Whether you're a fan of your baby going to various local play groups or not, it's worth knowing whether your little one will be out and about, or just in the house for the day. If there are playgroups, then ask if there are additional costs for these groups.

- **What kind of food and drink will you give?** It's definitely worth knowing what your child will be eating, how often they'll be fed and where they'll be fed. Ask to see the kitchen – check if it's clean, tidy and safe. Ask the childminder if they have a list of the foods they give to children.

- **How many other children do you look after?** At any one time, a childminder can care for a maximum of 6 children under the age of 8 (including their own children) and only 1 of these children can be under 1 year old. You'll want to know how many children will be present whilst the childminder is looking after your child. It's worth asking the age of the children too, so you get a better idea of the children your little one will be spending time with.

- **Do you have your own children?** Depending on whether this is important to you or not, you might want to ask if she has children of her own. It might be reassuring to know that the childminder understands what it's like to be a parent. Also, if her children are young and still live with her, then you're right to want to know who your baby will be spending their time with. Further, if the childminder is a mum, then she may have commitments such as school-runs.

- **Can we see your Ofsted registration number and your latest report?** All childminders need to be Ofsted registered. They might not have received a visit from Ofsted recently, but they will usually have been inspected within the first 30 months of practicing if they are on the Early Years Register. If they have been inspected previously then you can ask to see the Ofsted report or use the childminders Ofsted reference number to check the report online at reports.ofsted.gov.uk

- **Can we have a couple of references?** Don't be afraid to ask for references. Good childminders will expect parents to ask for references and will be more than happy to give them.

- **Why did you decide to become a childminder and how long have you been doing it?** Understanding what motivated the childminder to become a registered child-carer is a great way to lean a little bit more about them as an individual? Many will cite a love of children, but it's also quite common for there to be other motives, such as spending more time at home with their own children. If they say they love being with children, casually ask 'why?', so they can expand on what they really enjoy about being with children.

- **Do you do school pick-ups and drops?** This is good to know, not only with regards to which school or nursery your child goes to (and if they can pick up your child), but also to know how much time your child will be spend travelling between school pick-ups.

FINANCES

There are a number of ways childminders work on the finance front. Some are very business-savvy, whilst others might be a little more relaxed. I'm sure they'll all want paying; it's just that some are more flexible than others.

How much does a childminder cost?
Between £4.50 and £7.00 per hour - around £5 per hour is quite common in 2016. This'll be changing all the time and can vary quite a bit.

Do they want a retainer?
It was a surprise to us when we first heard of childminders requesting a retainer (non-refundable charge to you) for the period between when you agree terms (i.e. say that you want to use the childminder) to when your son or daughter actually starts going to the childminder. This retainer fee is commonly around 50%.

Are meals included?

You want to know if you're going to have to bring packed lunches and build this into the total cost of childcare. If the childminder does include lunch, ask to see the menu.

Holidays

How much notice do you (and the childminder) need to give for holidays?

When does the childminder usually take holidays? Can the childminder help with cover if she is on holiday or unable to look after your child? Do you have an alternative childcare option if the childminder isn't available?

Does the childminder expect to be paid during her holidays? How many holidays does the childminder take?

Do you still have to pay the childminder when you go on holiday? How much holiday are you allowed to take?

Sick leave

Similar to the questions on holidays, you want to know:

Does the childminder charge for when they are off sick?

Does the childminder charge for when your little one is off sick?

Many childminders don't charge for periods when they're off sick (although some do). In my experience it's common for childminders to still charge if your baby is off sick, otherwise they'd have a loss of earnings that they had no control over.

Are there late fees?

Most childminders will operate some sort of charge if you're late picking up your child. Some can charge quite hefty penalties, like £10 for every 10 minute period you're late! Other childminders might state that there are late fees in their contract, however, they understand that everyone can be late on rare occasions, so don't actually penalise you for arriving 5 minutes late to pick up your child. Although you might think you're never going to be late, it does happen to the best of us, so you want to get a feel for if the childminder is likely to sting you with a huge penalty for the one time you get stuck in traffic.

What's the termination period?
All good things come to an end, so find out how much notice both you and the childminder need to give before terminating the contract to end the childcare.

THINGS TO LOOK OUT FOR WHEN YOU VISIT A CHILDMINDER

Bring the family
Take your child along with you if possible, to see how the childminder interacts (or doesn't) with them. Does the childminder take an interest in your child? How does she talk to her? If the childminder isn't engaging with your little one, this isn't necessarily a sign that they're not a good child-carer; they might just be focussed on the conversation with you. It's also best if both parents come along so you can both get a feel for the childminder and the environment your little one will be moving in to. Having you both meet the childminder beforehand also tells the childminder that you're both involved and that the childminder should include both of you in communications.

Do a quick recce

Spend 5-10 seconds outside the house before you knock. Don't stand there looking all strange, but taking a few seconds to listen to what's going on inside the house before you enter could give you an idea of what the environment is like when you're not there. Is the childminder screaming expletives down the phone, or is she engaging happily with the children?

Is the house clean and safe?

Look for all the usual things here. Ask yourself: if this was your house, would you change anything (other than the decor) to make it more baby-friendly?

Is there a messy-play area?

Will your baby feel free to roam or be a bit constrained?

Is there a garden?

Depending on how important this is for you – you might want to consider if there's an outdoor space for your baby to play in during the warmer months.

11. BONDING WITH BABY

"They've got a teletepathic, teletephatic,
pathetic, well it's not pathetic...
oh just forget it"

Graham Taylor

This is a very difficult chapter for me to write. Why? Because every parent and every child is different – and what one dad may want to get out of fatherhood, or rather give in fatherhood, can differ hugely to another. For this reason, it's also probably the most important chapter for me personally to write – because I believe that how I approach parenting from the early stages will affect not only my relationship with my son or daughter, but their personality as well.

With this being a very personal experience, I proceed with caution. These are my own words and opinions only.

PROVIDE WHAT THEY NEED TO THRIVE

My dad once said to me, "I'll be happy, so long as you look back at me when I've passed away and say 'yea, my old man was alright'". Being a dad myself now, I truly get that sentiment. He knows that he hasn't, nay, couldn't be perfect – no father truly can. He needn't worry about whether he has been "alright" - "Dad, you're alright. And I love you.".

So far, I haven't considered, nor do I think I will consider, what I want my child to think about me. In one way, I feel it doesn't matter what they think about me. My goal as a dad is to provide my children with the guidance, love, support and nourishment they need to thrive as individuals. What they actually think of me is just a by-product and not the goal. How happy and fulfilled my children are, is all I think about.

How does that help me in my first year as a dad?
In the first year it might feel like you don't get much back in the way of conversation. Or it might feel like there is no way you can make

an impression on a tiny baby who can't walk or talk. Or it might even feel like you need to wait until your baby is a toddler or school-age before you can really come into your own and make a difference to their lives. In my opinion, the way you approach parenting from debut day onwards can have a profound impact on how you act as a parent in the years to come. I don't have any statistics to show you, I haven't looked. I feel that any statistics wouldn't change your mind one way or the other anyway. You'll either agree or disagree.

BEING WHAT MY BABY NEEDS ME TO BE

In terms of putting this approach into practice in the first year, here's a list of some obvious and perhaps less obvious dos, don'ts and behaviours I try to work by:

Provide what they need to thrive in the early months

This is actually quite easy. I mean, no, not the Being a Dad stuff, that's definitely not easy. I mean, it's easy to work on providing what a baby needs to thrive in the early months. Basically, get involved in the set pieces and spend time with them.

- A baby and mum will want to spend a lot of time together, and this is never more the case than in the first few months of a baby's life. Accommodate this by freeing up my partner from household tasks. In other words, do housework that needs to be done, without being asked to do it.

- Be active in the feeding process. If my partner is breast feeding then take the baby to her. If my partner expresses milk then get involved with the bottle feeding. A baby needs milk to survive, so associating myself with this most important of set pieces helps me build a closer bond with her.

- Accept that I can get frustrated and angry because my baby won't stop crying. At the same time, accept that this baby isn't trying to piss me off. Her crying is designed to grate on me so that I care for her.

- Spend time just cuddling my baby, without being on my phone or tablet at the same time.

...from the second half of the first season of fatherhood, I'll add...

- Accept that this is one hell of a confusing world for a baby, so accept that she will get frustrated with things (including me) and never take it personally. Repeat things to help her understand them.

- Empathise with my baby's frustrations and physically get down to her level (no matter how much this hurts my back). This shows I'm respecting her in both a psychological way and a physical way.

- Let her do things she is capable of (or thinks she is capable of). It might seem better to help her, but she'll learn to be independent if I give her the opportunity.

- If she has a small tumble but isn't hurt, then don't pick her up immediately. Help her learn to pick herself up.

- Tell her I love her, and show her I love her by looking after her and her mum.

- Let her explore her own world. Give her space and respect that she's her own person and will want to make her own decisions. Give her decisions to make. Starting with small things like what socks she can wear.

- Don't snatch things from her unless there is danger.

- Prepare her for change (i.e. talk about dinner a few minutes before dinner is ready and show her that dinner is ready, so that she can prepare to stop playing and join everyone at the table).

- Accept that she might not like people. Defend her right to dislike things.

- Avoid using the word 'shy' to describe my baby. She may have shy traits, but she's so much more than that and she shouldn't feel boxed in and defined.

- Lead by example. She'll do as I do, more than she'll do as I say.

- The most important thing for my child is love, so prioritise spending time with them instead of spending time on unimportant household jobs.

This isn't an exhaustive list – it's more of a collection of behaviours that I pledge to adopt. I feel a sense of fulfilment when act in this way, because I've helped both my partner and my baby, without expecting anything in return. My goal has never been about changing how they feel about me – I've never craved their gratitude. By simply helping my family, I feel fulfilled and happy. Being what they need me to be. Doing what they need me to do. You'll come up with your own ways of doing things. That's part of the fun of fatherhood.

WAYS TO BOND WITH YOUR BABY

There's a big pressure to feel an immediate unconditional love for your baby as soon as they exit the womb. The truth is, we don't live in Hollywood or an episode of Friends and it can take time to build a bond between dad and baby. In reality, when a newborn baby arrives, a new dad can experience any number of different feelings. He could feel elated, over the moon, apprehensive, calm, uneasy, empty, or even just relieved that mum and baby are both well. All these feelings (and many more) are completely normal and there isn't one way you're meant to feel, think or act. So whether you immediately fall in love with your baby, or feel that things aren't quite as natural as you expected, here are some things you could try to help build up a bond between your baby and you.

Cutting the cord – your first responsibility might be to cut the umbilical cord and this could help you adjust into your new role

Skin to skin – as you might expect, skin-to-skin literally means having your baby lay naked on your skin. It's common for mums to have skin-to-skin contact with their newborn baby soon after the labour. A multitude of research studies have shown that this can help babies to latch on, as well as having physical and psychological health benefits for the baby too. Dads are just as entitled to have a skin to skin contact with their little ones, so you could get half an hour of calm, with your baby nestled on your chest to kick off the bonding process. Try not to be concerned about the busyness of other mums, dads and midwives on the ward. Relax and just go with it. You might love it, or you might feel uneasy. If you think you might fancy doing it, then make sure to tell your partner before the day, so you can work it into any birth plans.

Put your face close to theirs - your face is the most fascinating thing for your baby to look at, and putting your face close to theirs helps them recognise you

Talk to your baby – they'll recognise the sound of your voice

Sing songs – which you used to sing to your baby when they were in the womb (if you did that)

Do the set pieces - feeds, nappy changes, bath time etc.

Plenty of cuddles

Read to your baby – from day one, reading helps your baby get familiar with your voice. Over the weeks and months to come, reading can help you build a routine and gives your baby all the benefits of early-stage reading. Reading also encourages you to spend quality time with the little one, instead of slipping off to do one of the many things that 'need to be done'

Get up in the night when they cry – it sounds strange to bring up crying as a time for bonding right? When your little one needs you, they cry. So being there for them, even through the difficult hours of the early morning, or when you're exhausted after work, tells them that a) you care about them, and b) both you and mum can look after them

Baby Massage – giving your baby a gentle back massage can help them relax. This works well at bath time.

Just the 2 of us – giving mum a rest and spending time with your baby on your own can be both fun and liberating. Small things like taking your baby to the park, or playing with a ball, can make a big difference.

FROM THE TERRACES

"*How long will it take before I have a connection with my baby?*"

This is a 'how long is a piece of string?' question. Whilst some dads will feel a big connection with their baby immediately, others take days, weeks or even months before they build a special bond. There's an overwhelming amount of new responsibilities to factor into your life, so you should forgive yourself if you don't have a connection with your little one for weeks or even months. It took me about a year before I felt a really strong connection with a) my little one, and b) defining myself as a dad..

"*When do you get immediate medical help?*"

I don't have an exhaustive list, but some symptoms that I would immediately get medical help from A&E or a doctor include a fit, bleeding in poo, not waking up, very floppy and weak, having a fit, breathing problems, very pale or blue skin, a temperature above 38C if my baby is under 3 months old, above 39C if she is 3 to 6 months old and above 40C if she is over 6 months old.

"What if I don't feel I have this connection?"

It can take months to build a bond between dad and baby. Even then, many dads feel that this early-stage bond isn't anywhere as strong as the bond that is built over the years to come. If you're concerned about your relationship with your baby, try speaking with a friend, relative or GP.

"How quickly can we communicate with our baby girl?"

Well you can start talking to her right away, but I wouldn't expect much response just yet. She's communicating with you from day 1 through her crying and by about 6-8 weeks babies usually start making a cooing or vowel sound.

12. THE BIG GAMES OF THE SEASON (BABY DEVELOPMENT)

"This squad is effectively a child learning to walk. We stumbled, we will do so again, but our fans are there to hold us up"

Claudio Ranieri

In this debut season, your little one develops massively – from a tiny newborn who'll only cry, sleep and feed, to a walking, talking little person with their own big personality. By the end of your debut season, you'll have dealt with more than you'd ever expected. From the brink of physically crashing out in the early months (you, not the baby), to end-of-season glory, here are the highlights and key milestones (no, key Big Games) of your first season with Dad F.C.

DAY 1–2 – KICK–OFF

Your baby has been through a big ordeal to get here. Don't be surprised if they chill out, just like their mum needs to. The main focus will probably be on ensuring that both mum and baby are getting plenty of rest, as well as giving your baby their first feeds. If your partner is breast-feeding then step one is to try to encourage your little one to latch on to her breast, this isn't always so easy. There'll be midwives on hand in these early stages to ensure both mum and baby are doing well.

WEEK 1 – SET PIECES

Taking set pieces and looking after your new family
Week one is all about getting familiar with the core set pieces: feeding, winding, changing and sleeping. There'll not be much in the way of human interaction for a while yet, so use this as an opportunity to take stock of the new member of the household and the impact they're already having on your life. Crying is your baby's main pasttime, so it might help if you try to learn their different cries – each cry will sound slightly differently depending on whether your baby needs feeding, changing, swaddling or is just plain tired.

You might be thinking about taking your baby for their first away game sometime at the end of week one. There are no rules on when you should take your baby out of the house for their first travels – just keep them warm and cosy (with a general rule being that your baby wears one more layer than you).
Your baby can just about make out a face, although everything they see is very blurry.

WEEK 2 – GETTING TO KNOW EACH OTHER

Your baby is built to let you know when they want something and it's your job to provide it
Your baby might get their first mini growth spurt around this time. You can bet that there'll be an increase in demand for milk when this happens. Your baby may spend increasingly more time awake, without really needing anything. It's easy to feel some guilt – like you should be doing something – even though your baby isn't demanding

anything. Try to ignore this feeling of guilt. There'll be plenty of time when they'll need you, so just enjoy spending time as a new family. It can feel unnatural to just sit and talk with a baby (after all, you won't get much back in the way of communication) but your baby will like the sound of your voice and may start to focus on your face.

For when your baby is crying, the usual suspects of feeding, sleeping, burping and changing continue to dominate proceedings. It's OK to pick your baby up when they start to cry, and you also shouldn't feel guilty if you decide to leave them to cry for a minute instead. Parents tend to want to get a perfect balance between a) tending to their baby's every whim and b) letting their baby self-soothe. Those are the 2 sides of the spectrum and there's rationale for both. Ultimately, babies are designed to let their parents know when they want something and it's the parent's job to provide it. Using common sense and gut-feeling will go a long way – where you sit on the spectrum of self-soothing (or not) is simply a matter of choice.

Colic may kick off
If your baby does get colic (intense bouts of crying) then they're more than likely going to get it around week 2. See chapter 9 for more info on dealing with colic. Remember, colic is no one's fault – your baby will need time and comfort.

WEEK 3 – RECOVERY ON TRACK

Mum is still recovering
This week, some dads may start to go back to work. This represents a big shift in the household: where dads may have taken the lion's share of new parental responsibilities up to this point, that's extremely difficult (dare I say impossible), if the dad is not at home. Try to get

involved in as many responsibilities as you can (the bedtime routine and weekends are great times to step in).

Mum will still be recovering from the labour, so is going to continue to need extra love and support. Most pregnancy and new baby books focus on the care and attention your partner needs before and during the birth. Truth be told, the first month (or months) after the birth can be even more challenging for a new mum, so you'll need to do more than your share of housework and baby set pieces (changing, winding, bottle feeding) as well as caring for your partner. This might sound like I'm stating the bleeding obvious, but it's duly worth noting.

You'll have another meeting with the health visitor at some point soon and they might talk through things like your baby's skin (which could have small white spots, baby acne or blotchiness – all of which are common) as well as your partner's health and wellbeing.

Your baby will continue to develop and will soon start focussing on your face (one of the big 'Firsts') that you'll really enjoy. They may be making more and more eye-contact with you.

What can she see, hear and think about?

Your baby has been hearing things since way back in the womb, so your voice is a comforting noise to her. She's been taking in the world around her, through what she sees, hears, smells and feels since day one. She won't really know what's going on or what everything means, but she will enjoy the familiar sound of your voice and getting to know who you are. It helps if you talk to your baby. When you're changing her, she might not feel comfortable with the cold air, but having a calm and talkative Dad can be very reassuring.

WEEK 4 – NOISES

Now that your baby is reaching the 1 month mark, she'll be able to lock her eyes onto bright colourful objects and watch you move objects from side to side.

Your baby will also start gurgling their first ummmm.... words?. You now have a tiny baby that can look at you in the eye and make baby-conversation! Such a great moment! Talk back to them and they'll love you for it!

Your little one is also ready for a bit of tummy time – where you lay them down on their front and watch as they try to lift their head, even for just a second or two.

MONTH 2 – SMILES AND SLEEPLESS NIGHTS

It's all smiles at Dad F.C.
One month or so into the season and your little one will start to show the signs of cheeky smiles. All those sleepless nights, baths, nappy changing and long feeds are well worth the moment your baby cracks their first smile. Thought they'd been smiling since day 1? No – that was just passing wind.

There are still night-time fixtures
You can still expect to be woken up a few times in the night – that's very common still at this early stage. If your little one is sleeping through the night then you're one of the lucky few. I despise you.

However, you could find that your baby is waking up fewer times in the night; having longer sleeps and longer periods of being awake.

Play-time begins in earnest

Your baby will increasingly jolt their arms and legs around more, as if they're warming up on the sidelines, waiting to be thrown onto the pitch. Their eyesight is still improving and they'll notice colourful mobiles and toys. Your baby will be more and more engaged with the world around them and will make weird and wonderful noises – so always talk to them about what you're doing (apart from at bedtime of course – you probably don't start conversations with them when you want them to sleep).

There'll be a check-up with your club doctor or nurse

As your baby has been out and about for a couple of months, it's time for their latest medical, which includes checking their weight, height, eyes, hips, heart, genitals and how they're feeding. Remember to take the red baby development book you were given at the hospital and also take this opportunity to ask your doctor or nurse any questions you may have about your little one. Your baby will also be offered immunisations this month.

MONTH 3 – BUILDING STRENGTH

So your baby probably now looks more like what you expected them to look like when they were born: a cute, chubby little monster that makes lots of fun noises and likes grabbing at things. Your baby will definitely be getting stronger now and may be keeping their head up for longer periods of time. Expect some little chuckles and they may be pushing down with their legs to hold weight. Babies are apparently born with the knowledge of how to walk – they just don't have the strength and ability to do it yet.

She will begin to know who you and her mum are, and don't be surprised if she favours being in her mum's arms more than yours. Who wouldn't? On the flip side, you might find that she's a daddy's girl. If she is a daddy's girl, definitely don't rub it in with mum – you'd just regret it.

Dad F.C. is a huge fan of reading, and even though your baby may not follow the plot to Wind in the Willows, reading from a young age is fantastic for both parent and child. Your little one will learn faster if you read to them, and you will enjoy watching them be entertained by your Jeremy Irons style narration.

A bedtime routine might start to come into play now, although you'll be lucky if you're not getting up in the nights for feeds still. Your baby may be sleeping for longer periods, but a consistent routine (same pretty much every night) might not start to happen for another 3-6 months. Rest assured (or 'lay awake assured') that a routine representing some sort of normality will kick in at some point.

MONTH 4 – IMPROVING SKILLS AND AWARENESS

Distraction / Diversion is a beautiful thing

You might be having difficulties with one or more of the set pieces. Maybe they love getting dressed in the morning, but absolutely detest bath-time. Maybe they love the bath but absolutely hate getting out. In the end, your baby will get used to the daily set pieces of feeding, winding, changing and bathing. Diversion can massively help when it comes to a tired and teary baby, so it's a skill that is really worth mastering. In one way or another, a great diversion tactic can work well for years. The best ways to divert a baby's attention are almost always the most obvious. Try completely changing your tone or act as if something has surprised you (then find an object to be 'surprised' about). Be pleasantly surprised and keep your tone soft, light and fun. You could also add a favourite toy into the mix, so that your baby is distracted by the toy, whilst you get them ready for the bath.

Raising themselves up

Your 3-4 month old won't quite be mobile yet, but will be able to raise themselves up onto their arms if placed face-down for tummy time exercises.

Bigger feeds, less often

Like sleep, your baby will be getting in more feeds, but less often. It's not time to start on solids yet; so long as your baby is happy and gaining weight then let the number of feeds naturally reduce whilst the size of the feeds grow over the coming weeks and months.

Dribbling skills improve

A sign of teething is that your baby starts to dribble more. Teething may start around 4 months, although you probably won't see a tooth for another couple of months.

Shirt-pulling

You'll see that your baby is really starting to get involved with the things around her now - if you put various toys in front her, she may pick them up, shake them or simply stare at them for a few minutes. She'll start grabbing at things too – she is now at a great age to get the play mats out and watch her bat at the bells and bash at the balls.

Seeing red

At 4 months your baby will be able to see the difference between brightly coloured objects (like primary colours) and tell the difference between similar shades, such as the blue and purple. Don't expect them to be able to tell the difference between a Liverpool and Manchester United kit for a few years yet.

MONTH 5 – HAVING A LAUGH

Who are ya?

Your baby may now react to their name now, as well as be able to decipher between new and familiar sounds. She might be used to hearing the clocks ticking, so she knows to ignore that sound, but take her outside and she'll turn her head if she hears a crow caw.

Pull a silly Dad Face

Your baby's mental development is stepping up a notch which means you can introduce the Dad-Faces that have been warming up. Start making silly noises and playing 'peek a boo' and your baby may laugh at how ridiculous dad has become.

The need for attention

They'll now be well aware of your presence in the room, so therefore equally aware when you're not in the room. Your baby is starting to realise they are their own person (not just an extension of their mum) so expect them to demand affection as they make sense of this ever-changing world they live in.

Put pillows all around them

At 5 months, your baby's physical development is also coming along at a rate of knots, so they might be able to sit up on their own (once you've propped them up with a few cushions).

MONTH 6 – TEETHING AND SOLIDS

Teething

At the mid-way point in the first season, your baby's first teeth may start to come through. This can scupper the bedtime routine that you'd just nailed. That's a shame. On the plus side, it's now time to brush that single tooth.

Starting on solids

One of the biggest games of the season (and one that you're sure to remember) is when your baby tries their first solids. You'll know that they're ready to try some solid foods when they're shoving their fingers in their mouth or jealously watching you tuck into your roast dinner. For good ideas on first foods to try, check out chapter 5 on Baby v. Food.

More rolling-over than Ronaldo

Your baby could be rolling over by now – which is a sign that they'll be starting to crawl in the coming months. The first rolls are a Big

Game of the Season. They also mean that you should start thinking about baby-proofing the house as it won't be long before your baby starts exploring.

Getting clever

Your baby now knows that they are an individual. They can communicate in more ways than just crying, so they'll begin to exercise this newfound freedom. They'll work out that if they cry, you react in a certain way. If they shout, you react in another way, and that if they stick something they shouldn't in their mouth, you'll react in a whole other way altogether.

6 month check-up

At 6 months your baby will get a complete physical examination from the doctor, including an assessment of their height, weight, heart, lungs, eyes, ears, mouth, head, body, genitals, hips and limbs. Your baby will also be offered their vaccinations and you'll probably be asked about their feeding, walking and holding skills. All babies develop at different times and no two babies are the same.

Continue reading

Little ones are now developing their own sounds and will begin to recognise the words they normally hear. Pointing at words and pictures when you're reading to them helps them match words to images and also helps develop their language skills.

MONTH 7 – REPEAT, REPEAT, REPEAT

Nursery rhymes (on loop)

By around month 7, you could find that you're continually singing 'round and round the garden, like a teddy bear'. The moment you stop, a certain little person demands that it's sung again. These little games on loop are actually a great way for your baby to learn and they'll love the repetition. Knowing what's coming up next is a new thing for your baby so it'll give them a sense of security and control over their tiny world.

Look who's talking?

Whilst there'll not be a proper conversation for a while yet, your baby might want to communicate with more than just a 'mo' or 'ba'. The first wave hello and goodbye may surface in the next few weeks or months.

Try a teether or teething ring

When your baby is cutting her first teeth, she might be interested in trying out a teether or teething ring to gnaw at.

On the move

Your little one might show more and more signs that they're ready to explore the world around them, as their gross motor skills (movement of her arms and legs for crawling) develop. They'll show an interest in anything remotely dangerous and you won't be able to take your eyes off them. They'll be creating their master plans of destruction for when they can crawl. You'll get cold sweats at least once a day as they surprise you with new ways to put themselves in harm's way. They'll be bouncing now: hold your baby under her arms and let her push her legs against your lap. Babies may also be able to sit up on their own now too.

It's like talking to a brick wall

If your baby doesn't seem to be listening to you, it's most definitely because you're going to ask them to do something they don't want to do. From a young age, they clearly develop the same sense of selective hearing that'll see them well into their teens. If you need to remove something from your baby's little mitts and they're being completely unresponsive to your pleas, try using the diversion tactics and definitely try not to get frustrated. Although it may feel like it, your baby isn't trying to piss you off intentionally... honest.

MONTH 8 – CRAWLING?

The crawling may well get under way from month 8 (although this might not happen for a while yet, so don't get upset or concerned if things are taking a little longer). Every baby develops at their own pace and you'll resent yourself when she actually does start crawling and you're running around baby-proofing the entire house.

There'll be more conversation now; your baby may start to give names for things. These names will be more of a sound than a word – like 'ba', for instance, which your baby uses to describe anything from 'bath' to 'banana'. But who cares? These are their first words and are a great reason to celebrate!

Is my little one developing OK?

It's completely normal to benchmark your baby with the baby of the mum at playgroup, your workmate's kid (who is already potty trained and reciting War and Peace... apparently) or with those passive-aggressive parents who frequent popular mum forums. Don't bother comparing. Babies like to take their own time and tend to accomplish their Big Games of the Season to their own timescale. If you have any concerns about your baby's development then speak to a doctor or health care visitor.

MONTH 9 – MORE FOOD. MAYBE MORE 'NO'S

At 9 months your baby will start to respond a little more to your requests – and your requests may often be 'Noooo'. Give as much encouragement and positive reinforcement as you can. It's very difficult to stop yourself saying 'No' and in actual fact, there's nothing wrong with the word. Just back it up with rationale (as you might do when saying 'no' to an adult) and avoid angry tones (as you might not do when saying 'no' to an adult'). When your little one is receptive to your requests, you could thank or praise them to encourage the behaviour.

You might find that your baby is getting more engaged with other babies now, so it's a good time to get out and about to try to meet up with other dads. Drop that other new dad at work an email to organise that play-date you always said you'd sort out.

To coincide with the insatiable appetite for more play-time, your little one may drop one of their afternoon naps – so expect relative adjustments to the night-time routine if this happens.

On the food front, continue to introduce new solids (unless they're still just on breast milk).

MONTH 10 – IMPROVING CORE STRENGTH AND VOCAB

A baby's vocabulary continues to progress now. Whilst they don't always put their mouth in gear, the words and phrases you commonly use are sinking into their sponge-like minds.

There'll be sitting-up more easily and might even be able to stand without support. Expect them to begin navigating their way around their newfound domain. Crawling becomes child's play, literally.

Babies can really express their individuality by now – showing a like or dislike for people, for no apparent reason, and throwing tantrums at their disdain for daddy-cooked dinner.

MONTH 11 – BOOKS AND TANTRUMS

"Rooney was complaining all the time, protests and more protests. He reminded me of my kids."

Referee Horacio Elizondo

If they're still not listening to a word you say, then that's fine. It's OK to repeat 'No', just try to be consistent, back it up with the reason why it's a 'No' and be relative – don't throw a tantrum yourself if your baby isn't doing what you think they should be doing. Be calm and patient – your baby needs to know that you're strong for them and that you can handle their inconsistencies.

Your baby may be taking their first steps anytime around now, so get ready for the Biggest Game of the Season! You can support them in their progress, by walking with them hand-in-hand to help with their balance.

At nearly One Year Old, a baby's fondness for books continues to grow, so get the shelves stacked with a good variety. Reading to your baby every day is one of the simplest yet most powerful habits you can adopt.

Note to self: organise the first birthday party.

MONTH 12 – FIRST STEPS?

A baby's first steps might come around about now (if they haven't already). With new found freedom comes much responsibility. Two, often overlooked, potential side-effects of starting to walk are 1) a baby's appetite may grow to accommodate all the extra energy needed for running around, and 2) your baby has just realised their biggest Gross Motor development – walking is a bigger change for them than it is for you. Don't be surprised if they experience bouts of anxiety as they adjust and accept their independence.

A 12 month old can make a lot of noise. They can enjoy squealing, banging pots and pans together and they tend to get some sadistic pleasure from smashing the Duplo tower you had cleverly crafted to completion moments earlier.

You're here. Boom. Well done on getting to the end of the first season with both you and your baby in one piece.

13. WIN IT LIKE LEICESTER CITY

"Every minute of hard work we've put in ... has been worth it..."

Jamie Vardy

The 2015-2016 football season saw the big outsiders, Leicester City win the Premier League for the first time in their history. The Foxes were tipped for relegation before the season began and the bookies were so sure that they wouldn't win the league that they offered odds of 5,000 / 1 if Leicester did go all the away. And the rest, as they say, is history.

New Leicester City manager Claudio Ranieri went from an uninspiring underachiever – Gary Lineker famously tweeted "Claudio Ranieri? Really?" upon the Tinker Man's arrival at the King Power stadium – to a full-blown football legend in his debut season at the club.

The First Season of Fatherhood has many similar challenges to those faced by King Claudio in his first season. So let's take a look at exactly what happened at Leicester, because there are a few (tenuous) comparisons that can be drawn...

Survival was key for Leicester
Like Leicester, dads don't plan to be amazing. Just surviving the first year is mission accomplished.

Leicester City accepted that they weren't the best team in the league
The best dads know that they aren't the best dads – they just try to be as good as they can be for their children.

Leicester built a team on a shoe-string and then got the best out of it
Dads have to be just as lean...
- Accept freebies: Marc Albrighton was offloaded by Aston Villa. Fuchs, Wasilewski Schlupp, King and Schwarzer all

also cost absolutely nothing
- Accept loans: Nathan Dyer was on loan from Swansea City
- Accept hand-me-downs: Robert Huth, Mark Schwarzer (both former Chelsea), Danny Simpson, Danny Drinkwater, Matty James (all former Manchester United), Kasper Schmeichel (former Manchester City). These 6 players cost Leicester City a total of around £8 million, the same amount Manchester City paid for Fabien Delph

Leicester's main striker was plucked from non-league minnows Fleetwood Town.

New dads always start from scratch and work their way up the parenting ladder – with no experience of the big league.

Leicester started the season winning just 3 of their first 7 games, conceding 14 goals in the process (hardly title winning form).

There is no ultimate guide to being a parent (even this book surprisingly won't teach you how to be a parent). When dads make their debuts, they can be all over the place, making any number of errors.

Leicester played for pizzas

Like Ranieri rewarding player's with pizzas for keeping clean sheets, dads learn to enjoy the small things in life. It's one single beer at home rather than a night out with the lads. It's a takeaway rather than a fancy restaurant.

It was 10 games (over 2 months) before Leicester kept a clean sheet

You'll struggle to keep clean sheets too. There will be more laundry to do than you could ever have imagined.

Vardy broke a Premier League record by scoring in 11 consecutive games

Dads break their own personal record of having no sleep for 11 consecutive nights.

Leicester City used fewer players than any other Premier League team

Dads wear fewer shirts than they've ever worn before in order to save time, effort on laundry.

The club had a great team spirit

Dads need to have the same camaraderie with mums – we're in this together

Leicester's players played with a smile on their faces

Things can get very tough being a new dad. There can be a lot of pressure to handle, so embracing things with a positive attitude can help get dads to the top.

Leicester City suffered hiccups (last-minute loss to Arsenal) and the red mist descended (Vardy got sent off in the draw vs. West Ham)

There'll be times when all dads get frustrated and fall off course. We are only human after all.

There was a strong fan base at Leicester

Leicester supporters' celebrations were captured on the Richter scale, causing a small earthquake, when Leonardo Ulloa scored a last-minute winner against Norwich. Knowing you have support from others to call upon is a tremendous help to new parents.

Leicester's player didn't get paid extra for winning the league!

Being a dad is the toughest job in the world and you don't get paid for it. In the world of overpaid footballers, it's refreshing to know that the Leicester City players didn't get any additional bonus for finishing higher than 12th in the league.

It was all a miracle
The chances of nurturing that specific 1 in 100 million sperm into a fully-fledged 1 year old are pretty slim, but we're confident you'll get them there. Dad FC is not big on the science part, as you have probably gathered yourself.

The reward is humongous!
The feeling dads get from seeing their baby grow-up is amazing. There is truly nothing like it.

THE FINAL WHISTLE

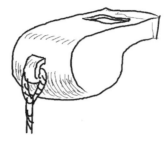

So, in much the same way that Claudio Ranieri won the Premier League with Leicester City in 2016, we hope that this book contributes to helping you have a successful debut season in fatherhood. All new dads suffer a few setbacks along the way (we're only human); it's how we overcome these setbacks really that matters. So practice your set pieces, look after mum, get your hands dirty (a lot) and most importantly... enjoy this special time with your family.

Thanks for reading
Dad FC's Debut Dads – The First Season of Fatherhood

Good luck!
Alex

www.dadfc.com
www.facebook.com/DadFC

NOTES

NOTES

Printed in Great Britain
by Amazon

69981992R00127